Pearls

Pearls

*A Memoir On Childhood Brain Cancer
and Hope*

Maggie Bushway

Rob Bushway

Contents

Preface   xi

Introduction   xiii

Part One
Irritation

1. Fearless   3
2. Petrified   5
3. The Day Everything Changed   8
4. Thanksgiving   18
5. Siblings   24
6. Chemo   32
7. Friends   42
8. Faith Like a Child   51
9. Brave   59
10. Radiation   63
11. Stages   69
12. Remission   75

Part Two
Convalescence

13. The Calm Before the Storm   81
14. The Storm   86
15. Temporal Lobectomy   92
16. Seizures   101
17. St. Louis   105
18. Foreshocks   123
19. The Earthquake Pt. 1   131
20. The Earthquake Pt. 2   144
21. Faith Like an Adult   152
22. Aftershocks   156

Part Three
Pearl Formation

23. Chronic   163
24. Am I Weak Enough Yet?   174

Afterword   177
Acknowledgments   179
About the Author   181

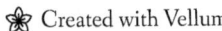

Dedicated to Little Maggie, whose dream was to publish this book someday.

Preface

I wanted to write my story 20 years ago, at age 8. There was no way that I could have done that effectively at that age and in the middle of cancer treatment. My dad, Rob, unknowingly was telling my story on his blog, but it was still missing my perspective. Looking back, I have an overall perspective, but there are memories that are hazy and details that I've forgotten.

This story wasn't mine alone. It was a journey my entire family walked together. None of us have the full picture. Each of us have a piece of the puzzle, and the process of writing this book put the puzzle pieces together.

The layout is unique, in that parts of it portray the child-like idea of a writing a book, including how a child would illustrate it. My dad's blog posts are a large part of the book. I also include quotes from my mom, Kathi, and siblings: Dax, Anna Kathryn, and Zoe. Each perspective is separated by a pearl. This is our story, woven together from the threads of our individual experiences.

Rob: God uses Love to knit together so many different aspects of pain, that when you stand back to look at the quilt He has woven, you don't see the threads of pain. Instead, you see patchworks of Grace, Goodness, and Kindness – patchworks that represent His Body.

Introduction

I always wanted to be a writer. From the moment I understood what a story consisted of, I knew I wanted to spend the rest of my life telling stories. At 7 years old, I wrote an innocent story about two bunnies. Not even a year later, my writing changed drastically when I began writing about my journey with childhood brain cancer. At such a young age, I didn't know how to articulate what was happening to me, but I sure did try. My dream was to publish a book about my cancer experience from start to finish and how God got me through it. I survived cancer, but surviving cancer has long-lasting consequences. I've been waiting this whole time to finish it for me to get to a place where I could look back with perspective, with a healed brain and body, and tell a story that wraps up nicely and feels good. My matured view on stories is that it's not always about the hero conquering the big, scary tumor, being seizure-free, and coming out the other side unscathed. Sometimes it's about finding peace where I am and realizing that maybe God is using me as a plot point in His story. With this mindset, I am finishing my story alongside my 8-

year-old self and with my dad, Rob. Little did I know, he was chronicling it on his blog and through journaling. My mom and siblings provided their perspectives, looking back.

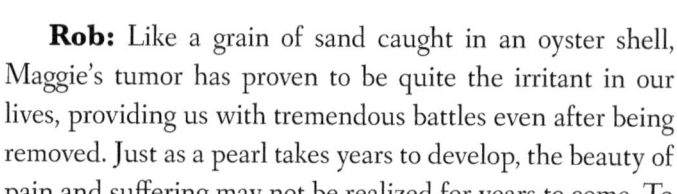

Rob: Like a grain of sand caught in an oyster shell, Maggie's tumor has proven to be quite the irritant in our lives, providing us with tremendous battles even after being removed. Just as a pearl takes years to develop, the beauty of pain and suffering may not be realized for years to come. To fix the irritation or wish it away, will rob you of the joy of seeing the pearl of God's priceless purpose in it all.

Little Maggie: If you are sick like me you might want to hear the rest of the story. Even if you're not a Christian, I think what you hear will help you.

———————•○•———————

dAddy　　Mommy　　dAx　　Maggie　　Anna Kathryn　zOe

Part One

Irritation

Chapter 1

Fearless

Even as a baby, I always had health issues. I had terrible reflux and would scream inconsolably, tearing my tied tongue. Some babies just do that, but my doctors later wondered if it was more than reflux. My brother, Dax, and I were born in Meridian, Mississippi. Two years later, we moved to Colorado Springs, where I grew up. As a toddler, I would randomly turn blue due to lack of oxygen. After I got my tonsils out and started using a CPAP at night, my condition improved, and I grew out of it. I look back on the following three years as if they were from a utopian novel.

I loved food more than anyone else in the house. As my mom tells it, when I walked, the ground shook. I remember standing on the table after dinner and walking over to everyone's plates to eat their leftovers. Sweet potatoes were my favorite, (and still are).

My sisters were born and added so much joy to our lives. Our parents raised us as Christians and homeschooled us. They didn't decide this based on religion but because it was my mom's dream to homeschool us. She wanted to be more involved in our lives and spend as much time as possible with us. This decision helped us develop a bond as siblings that I'd treasure my whole life.

While my mom was teaching Dax to read, I was four years old, "playing" under the table, but learning to read as well. I soon did this with all his subjects and would even answer on his behalf, infuriating Dax. My mom started school with me, too, because I wanted to learn. I quickly picked up everything from reading and writing to math.

School wasn't the only thing I enjoyed. I had a full social life, including playing with my neighbors, Ariana and Ashley. They were my age, and we grew up side by side. I was also a little daredevil, in ways that horrified my parents. I often climbed the fireplace mantel and did flips off it. Another time, I climbed to the top of the swing set and walked across it like a balance beam.

The last clear memory I have before our lives would forever change really paints a picture of the playful relationship I had with my siblings. People think of cold weather when they think of Colorado, but just as our winters were intense, so was the summer heat. As children, my sisters and I were always looking for ways to escape the relentless sun. One summer, we stumbled upon a simple yet brilliant idea that would become one of our fondest childhood memories —Color City. It all began with a discovery: if we sprayed our chalk drawings with the water hose, the vibrant colors would blend and swirl, turning the once hot and dry pavement into a thin layer of cool and colorful mud. Excited by this discovery, we wasted no time in covering the entire back porch in chalk designs, our imaginations running wild. The transition from Color City to living in shades of gray for years to follow, was something I didn't even notice until my life became colorful again.

Chapter 2

Petrified

By six-years-old I was exceeding in all areas of life, but especially school. Halfway through second grade, I all of a sudden stopped. It was as if I just unlearned everything from the past two years. My mom assumed it must be that she wasn't teaching me well enough, but soon I began to change in other ways.

One morning I was playing with my dolls in the living room by our big window, looking out to the neighborhood. Our neighborhood was always alive and active, full of people of all ages out and about. It wasn't out of the ordinary for people to be walking their dogs during the day, but that morning, the sight of the dog on a leash petrified me. I just knew it was going to escape the leash, bolt towards the house, break through the windows, and eat me. I cried and hid under the window so that the dog wouldn't see me.

It could be anything that would set it off. According to my mom, we were going to the grocery store one day and a police car passed by us. The sound of its siren made me scream in terror. It wasn't even that the siren meant that there was a crisis, it was the sound that made me afraid.

Another time, my dad was grilling hamburgers and hot dogs, another common thing at our house. One minute, I was playing outside with Dax, Anna Kathryn, and Zoe, looking forward to my hot dog. In a split second, I was convinced that that tiny flame was going to spread across the porch, to the house, burn it down, and that we'd all die. I ran as far away from the house as I could get in our back yard. Nobody could convince me I was safe.

I began to assume what I was doing while having these terror attacks caused them, and therefore refused to do that activity, wear those clothes, or eat that food. It wasn't defiance, I was truly trying to protect myself, but couldn't communicate why I felt afraid of things. I would often have these terror attacks when eating, making me feel nauseous and couldn't finish my meals, or eat that food altogether anymore. This safety tactic became isolating, and from the outside seemed like a behavioral issue to some doctors. My primary pediatric doctor, Dr. Kautz, was certain that it wasn't a behavioral or environmental issue because he saw us so often and how we interacted with each other. He sent us to every "ologist" that you could think of, including a neurologist, who said he wanted an MRI but didn't think I could handle it.

We went to church with a pediatrician who specialized in developmental disorders, and she offered to see me. My mom carried me into her office wrapped in a towel. I shivered so often that my parents thought I was cold, so they always had me in a blanket or towel. The doctor immediately recognized that I was having seizures. She knew exactly what was wrong, but wanted to get an MRI before telling my parents their worst nightmare.

Little Maggie: Have you ever been so scared but you can't talk to people about how you feel? Like, example: at the dentist if your mouth is open and the dentist is working on you and you feel feel really scared and you really want to talk to your mom and dad but you can't talk while your mouth is open. I know how you feel.

Chapter 3

The Day Everything Changed

The first time in an MRI machine is scary for anyone, but especially a child. It made different banging noises and sounded like something was in the machine with me. I don't blame the neurologist who didn't get an MRI sooner; I don't know how I got through this scan. It was purely by the grace of God that I remained still enough for the machine to capture what it needed to.

———— •○• ————

August 21, 2003

Rob: We learned today, through an MRI, that Maggie has a mass of about 14mm x 11mm in size, located on top of her pineal gland. We don't know whether this is a cyst or a tumor. But given the size and Maggie's age (7), the doctors are very concerned. It is common for people to have pineal cysts, but not of this size and not at such a young age.

There was another finding indicating some damage on her brain where Maggie has had a problem with hypoxia (lack of oxygen). We are seeing a neurosurgeon on Friday morning at 8:00 a.m. to go over the findings in more detail and determine the nature of this mass. The neurosurgeon who is seeing us tomorrow is normally off on Fridays, but insisted on seeing us first thing on Friday. We will send out an update on Friday after we meet with the doctor. Please pray for Maggie.

My grandma went with us to the neurologist's office that day. While my parents spent hours with him, being told that their 7-year-old daughter had at least one rare brain tumor and would need emergency surgery, I was playing with toys in the waiting room with my grandma, who was trying her hardest to hold it together for me.

Rob: As I walked out of the doctor's office, my head reeled with information overload. Tears threatened, and I felt sick to my stomach. Life as I knew it had just changed.

The way home was very quiet as my parents processed what they just heard. I had no concept of the severity of the situation, but I could feel a serious tone in the car. I was looking out the window and pointed out that the cars were moving backwards, trying to lighten the mood. Looking back, it's clear I was hallucinating. Even though everything terrified me, I didn't know what to be afraid of in this situation.

Rob: With Maggie and Kathi in the van with me, I pulled over to call my pastor. I got out of the van and sat on the side of the road - "Maggie has a brain tumor, possibly two, and it doesn't look good at all," I began. Then I broke down, sobbing.

We pulled over at one point and my dad got out of the car, clearly upset. I'd never seen him break down like this before, and it was then that I realized that this must be a very big deal. Did I know what a tumor was? Or cancer? No. But I knew that if my dad was sad, he had reason to be.

Rob: After praying with my pastor, I hung up the phone and wept uncontrollably. I had only cried like that one time before, and it was at my Grandfather's funeral. Now my seven-year-old little girl was about to meet God and walk with Him in a way that most people will never experience. I was scared for her, I was afraid for my family, and I knew I didn't have the strength to fight this battle.

———— •◯• ————

People talk about how it must have been so hard for me to go through this at such a young age, but honestly I think it was much harder for my parents. Being fully aware is so much more painful than being unaware of the severity of the cancer that had just invaded our life. Thankfully they didn't know the full extent of what our journey would look like, but they knew enough. Now, being just a few years younger than they were at the time, I can't imagine the strength and faith it took for them to make the decisions they were about to make.

———— •◯• ————

Rob: I don't know how long I sat on the side of the road. But I knew I didn't want to get back in that van. In that van lurked a major crisis that I was not equipped to handle. But I also knew my wife and daughter desperately needed me. From the curb, I looked into Kathi's eyes. They said it all: Hurt, scared, angry, and needing some strength.

———— •◯• ————

Kathi: I remember thinking, I don't want 3 kids. I want 4. The only thing I remember saying to God that day was "Please give me grace. Help me turn around and smile at her. Help me talk to her without crying or throwing up."

When my dad got back in the car he seemed a bit more calm but still very sad. We continued the ride home, all terrified of the unknown. My other doctor appointments hadn't gone like this. Usually they were disappointed at the lack of answers, but not in shock.

Rob: Back in the van and driving home, I could hardly see where I was going from tears streaming down my face. Cars melded into each other. Two lanes became one. Grasping for anything I could get my hands on, I picked up a fast-food cup and slammed it against the windshield. Kathi gently touched my hand, and looked desperately into my shaking face. She knew.

Maggie sat quietly in the back seat – alone, knowing something was terribly wrong. I can only imagine what was going through her precious mind. Her "strength" and "care" were in the front seat falling apart in front of her.

None of us said much from the time we walked out of the doctor's office until we got home. As I pulled up to the house and opened the garage door, the reality of what just happened was beginning to hit home. This crisis was now invading our home.

We returned home to break the news to my 3 siblings: 8-year-old Dax, 3-year-old Anna Kathryn, and 2-year-old Zoe. I'm sure they had been blissfully playing, unaware that their whole world was about to flip upside down. When my parents explained to my siblings what was going on, it was the first time I heard it explained in words I could understand. My dad told us that I am very sick with a brain tumor, and that we would be spending a lot of time going to the doctor, maybe even a few a week. What shocked all of us children was that I'd have to go to the doctor that often. In our old world, children really only went to the doctor for yearly checkups. We had no idea how much more often it would really be, that we'd practically be living at the doctor's office.

———————○•———————

Rob: Fear and the unknown would dominate much of their lives for the next three years. They would need me to be their anchor in this storm.

———————○•———————

Kathi: I don't remember putting the kids to bed that night. I do remember Rob lying in Maggie's bed, crying and holding her as she slept, sometimes waking up with seizures. I remember thinking "these kinds of things don't happen to people like us. Things like this happen to those other people, far away."

Soon after talking to my siblings, we hugged them good-bye, leaving them in the care of our neighbors, and left for the children's hospital in Denver for emergency surgery. We urgently drove 2 hours to the hospital, as if death would beat us there.

Rob: We were on our way to Denver to talk to some surgeons. Maggie asked me, "Am I going to be OK?" I had to tell her that I didn't know. The look on Maggie's face still pierces my heart. The closest thing I can relate it to is to tell your family that their sibling had just died.

When we arrived and saw the surgeon expecting us, he told us that there's been a mistake and I did not have a brain tumor after all, but two cysts. He told us that children don't get tumors in the insular cortex. And I wasn't experiencing seizures, just migraines. After the 24 hours we'd just had, of course this was good news, but what were we supposed to do with that?

Little Maggie: The doctors found a tumor in my brain, so I had brain cancer, and when we went home that day, we went to the emergency room. I was going to have surgery, but then the doctor came in and said I didn't have a brain tumor, so we went home and we were all really happy and even though it was dark, we played outside.

We had emotional whiplash, going from being afraid for my life to celebrating. But I deep down felt a sense of dread. And I felt guilty for thinking that they were wrong, but the medicine wasn't helping and I could tell there was something bigger going on here. But I was 7, I didn't know anything. Though I didn't know at the time, my parents felt the sense of dread too. It felt illegal to celebrate and illegal to not celebrate at the same time. So we played outside in the dark.

Little Maggie: I knew when the doctors told my mommy and daddy that I didn't have cancer, that they were wrong. I knew that something was wrong with me and that I was just going to have to wait until they found it.

Chapter 4

Thanksgiving

I didn't realize it at the time, but my parents also didn't believe that I was perfectly fine. My mom called the doctor in Denver repeatedly, telling him that she was concerned about how I was doing and begging him to dig deeper. I was only getting sicker, and the brain surgeon drilled it into our heads that we should just be happy that it's not a brain tumor and that I don't have cancer.

———•○•———

Little Maggie: The doctor said I was all well and it was just a cyst. I thought maybe the doctor was wrong and they'd have to do something. They said I should be happy and that it would make me feel better, but it's hard to be happy when I'm not feeling good. Sometimes all I can do is lie in bed. I try to be happy but then a seizure starts and that makes me so scared.

Several months passed, and the migraine medicine prescribed was doing nothing. I continued having seizures and the mass continued to grow. The doctors suggested getting another scan 3 months later to see if there were any changes.

After getting the scan, we went on a trip to Horn Creek, Colorado. This was the last "normal" thing we did as a family for a while. My parents got a call on this trip that the mass had grown. I'm sure they felt very helpless being out of town while hearing this information. There was a doctor who was also there with her family at Horn Creek, and advised my parents to get some more eyes on my scans.

When we returned, there was a lot of politics and debate among doctors about what the mass is and why it's growing. The doctor in Denver who saw me before, was insistent that he wasn't wrong. Other doctors were sure it was a tumor and it needed to come out. A neurosurgeon at that same hospital got a hold of my scans and was alarmed by my diagnosis and treatment plan. He asked us to come back and schedule surgery because he was sure it was a tumor, though this still didn't convince my previous surgeon. With just one phone call our bubble popped and we were right back in the eye of the storm. My first diagnosis was correct, after all.

We scheduled surgery for a week or two out, and tried to prepare ourselves. Both sets of my grandparents were in town, and would be helping out with my siblings. It was Thanksgiving week, and I'd be in the hospital all week, so we celebrated early.

Rob: November 18, 2003

Update before Maggie's first brain surgery:

Dear Friends:

As Maggie's surgery date gets closer, the reality of what she will be going through becomes more real and heavy. I would be lying if I didn't acknowledge that it has caused and is causing a great deal of anxiety and worry for all of us, in different ways.

For Maggie, she worries about getting an IV and that her friends are OK. She has greatly improved while on the anti-seizure medicine. This is very good as it tells the doctors that they are doing the right thing by removing the tumor.

For Kathi, it has been an especially difficult week as she is almost always on the verge of tears.

For Dax, he struggles with all the attention that Maggie is getting, but at the same time readily acknowledges that this is in God's hands. While waiting to pick up our Cub Scout popcorn, Dax and I were talking about Maggie. I asked him how he is doing with all of this. He replied "I'm really not too worried about it. I mean, I do worry and that sometimes can't be helped. But this is in God's hands. Every now and then I worry about her and that is OK, but then I remember God is in control."

For our little ones, Anna Kathryn and Zoe, they let us know that they need our attention as well. For me, I struggle with keeping a clear head, so I can think and lead our family clearly through the path God has laid before us.

We had to go to the hospital a few days in advance for pre-op. To make me more comfortable, I brought my friend, Ashley. They had a doll on the operating table and pretended to put it to sleep so that I'd understand what would happen. When it was time for my actual surgery, Dax would be there instead of Ashley. Knowing there would be familiar faces there gave me so much peace.

For the first time in what would be many times, I fasted the night before my surgery. What I didn't know was that early the next morning, the waiting room was packed full of friends and family who fasted with me and showed up to support a young cancer patient. I remember my parents telling me that everyone was doing that, and I felt a lot less alone, though I was pretty concerned that nobody else ate breakfast. They must have been just as hungry as I was.

Somebody gave me a turkey stuffed animal from the gift shop, and I would not let it go. I asked if it could go into surgery with me, and they assured me it would be with me the whole time. I was skeptical, but it made me a little less scared to have a friend there with me. When I woke up, I immediately felt around me and noticed my turkey was not there after all, and started to panic. The nurse knew what was wrong and picked up my turkey from the end of my bed. To me that's all I needed to know. I felt so relieved, unlike all of the adults.

Yes, they did get part of my tumor, but it was so deep in my brain that they couldn't remove all of it. This meant that my journey was about to get a whole lot more painful and drawn out than we could ever imagine.

I have this vivid memory of being in the pediatric unit that still makes me laugh. One nurse came in and I admired her bright blue stethoscope that honestly looked like a toy. She took it off and said it's mine. I played with it, but every time a doctor or nurse came in, they'd take it and put it away. I explained countless times that it was given to me, but nobody believed me, and kept putting it away. I somehow had it in my possession when I was discharged and still have it to this day. Shh, don't tell!

Like I said before, it was Thanksgiving week. That wasn't really on our radar anymore, that is until we had surprise visitors. Only family members were allowed to visit, but our next door neighbors, the Hoseys, were as close as family. That didn't count to the hospital staff, so they told a few white lies to get in and bring Thanksgiving dinner and my siblings to us. That was one of so many times this family would bless us by showing up and being there for us on this long road ahead of us.

Thanksgiving 2003 was the scariest Thanksgiving I remember. But we still had so much to be grateful for. By no means do you have to be grateful for brain cancer or surgery. But we were thankful for both sets of grandparents who came to love and support us. We were thankful that I got a diagnosis in time to treat it. We were thankful for our neighbors who spent the holiday in the hospital with us. We were thankful for my surgeon who removed as much as he could and knew when to stop, giving me a better quality of life. Most of all, we were thankful for the body of Christ that so quickly surrounded us and provided for us in ways we didn't even know we needed.

I stayed in the hospital for three days to recover from the surgery, which the staff said was irregularly quick. But apparently, the younger you are, the more resilient you are likely to be. None of us were thankful at the time for this happening to a 7-year-old, but looking back, I am thankful that it happened at a resilient age.

Chapter 5

Siblings

I think often about how young my sisters were; how young we all were, when I got sick. I had some memories that were untainted with cancer, but it was all my sisters knew. It was normal to Zoe to be nicknamed "Zofran," the anti-nausea drug that got me through chemo. Instead of going to daycare, they went to a special play-place at the chemo clinic for siblings of cancer patients. My brother was old enough to know that this was not normal.

---○---

Rob: November, 2003

I can tell you how it has affected Zoe, our youngest daughter. It was Zoe's birthday and as is the tradition in our family, the birthday person gets to choose where they want to go out to dinner. We asked Zoe where she would like to go and she replied, "Hmm, where do you think we can go that will be quiet enough for Maggie so that she doesn't shake?"

Just because we were going through our worst nightmare, it by no means meant that we didn't make room in our lives for fun. Sometimes I wonder what the whole experience would be like without Anna Kathryn and Zoe. There would have been a lot less laughter, that's for sure. As a family, we developed a dark sense of humor that's hard for others to understand if they haven't been through what we have.

One day Zoe went with me to a neurosurgery appointment that fell on Halloween. Of course we all dressed up. I was a clown, Anna Kathryn was a princess, but Zoe was a brain surgery patient. Her costume consisted of a Pull-Up on top of her head, resembling the bandage that she saw on my head after surgeries. It was sad that that's what Zoe was familiar enough with to dress up as, but we had to laugh. Zoe also had the idea to hide under the chemo clinic front desk with a wolf mask on, and scare the receptionist. She succeeded at this, and laughed about it for years.

After a long hospital stay, we took a trip to the dentist. This was almost fun because it was a "normal" type of appointment since it wasn't complicated and no matter what, it shouldn't reveal any life or death issues. We got through my appointment with no seizures, which was a huge win! I was waiting with my mom as Anna Kathryn was with the dentist, when the dentist came out and said there was a problem. Anna Kathryn was in anaphylactic shock. She was having an allergic reaction to the food coloring in the toothpaste. They gave her an Epipen, and we rushed to the doctor. I'll never forget hearing Zoe comforting Anna Kathryn on the way there by saying,

"Don't worry, if you have a tumor, I'll make you a card." We were so physically and emotionally spent from my treatments, and worried about Anna Kathryn, but all we could do in that moment was laugh. You have to be able to find the humor in those situations or else your world can become dark and hopeless.

Anna Kathryn is a calming and nurturing presence in our family. She was born 30-years-old and kept us all in line, yet an absolute joy to be around. We could be having the worst day, but when Anna Kathryn would walk in the room wearing her entire closet for a fashion show, you best believe we all turned our attention toward her as she provided a much needed distraction. When Zoe would be comedic relief, she knew it, which encouraged it all the more. But when Anna Kathryn was our comedic relief, she was 100% serious about whatever she was doing. God gave us my sisters to brighten our world.

———————•○•———————

Little Maggie: My sisters Anna Kathryn and Zoe are so funny. They laughed and played and tried to make me feel better.

Rob: December 1, 2004

When Maggie is feeling good, she is doing wonderfully, fully engaging with the rest of the family. When she is having some bad days, she sleeps a great deal. Emotionally, she is withdrawn and very tired. She had a rough day on Sunday as she struggled to see the other kids in her Sunday School class doing things very easily. She came home and cried — upset that she wasn't normal like the other kids and frustrated that she couldn't do her worksheets. Dax was with her after Sunday School to comfort her. Dax is such a great big brother and God is molding him into a man after His own heart.

———————○•———————

Dax has always been one of my best friends. Some of my favorite memories with him were playing chess late at night, or building a whole Lego city in his room, and then making up an ongoing storyline and consistent characters to play with every day. This changed some depending on my treatments and hospital stays, but I didn't feel like my friendship with Dax changed or that he would give up on trying to include me, no matter how sick I was. I know that he struggled with me changing from brain damage, but he never let it show to me.

———————○•———————

Rob: Dax asked the other day "when will Maggie be back? The Maggie I used to know and play with, my best friend. When are things going to return back to the way things used to be? I miss Maggie." We told him we didn't know "Maggie" would ever be back to the way she used to be, and that our family would never be the same. He choked up and pushed past his tears and said, "OK. That's all I needed to know."

Dax: Maggie had been sick for about a year. She wasn't getting much better and she was about to go through some major treatments. Being the oldest sibling, I took on a great deal of responsibility when Maggie was in the hospital.

Sometimes I wonder what our family would have been like if we didn't go through what we've been through. But I don't entertain that thought for long because I'm so thankful for how we are now. No, we never were the same; we're better off. Growing up, people were blown away finding out that we hardly ever fought and were thick as thieves. But can you blame us? The long amount of time I'd spent away from my siblings in the hospital, (sometimes out of state) made us cherish the time we had together all the more. Dax, Anna Kathryn, and Zoe grew closer, comforting each other and praying that I'd come home. Dax and I grew closer as he got to know and love a different version of Maggie. Anna Kathryn, Zoe, and I became closer as I didn't want to miss a chance to be a big sister to them when I could. We didn't grow tired of each other, knowing that each moment together was a gift.

Anna Kathryn: I think it's made me into the type of person that always feels the need to step up in any situation and try to problem-solve. It makes me thankful for each day we are given and to not take anything for granted.

Zoe: Anna Kathryn was my best friend growing up, and remains one of my best friends. We stuck by each other, and honestly, I don't know what I would've done without her with me during those times.

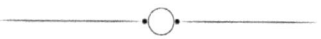

Dax: I don't fondly look back on the times in my childhood that Maggie wasn't a part of.

Consistently over the years, any time I would be in the hospital and feel depressed, it was always over not being with my siblings. The surgeries and treatments were hard, but we were all so close that it felt like parts of me were missing when I was away from my siblings. I didn't feel like myself without them.

Even as we're all adults now, what we've all been through still affects how we relate to those around us, and each other. Unsurprisingly, Dax is now a resident in Family Medicine. He still likes to be involved in and stay in-the-know about my medical care, and knows what to do in a crisis better than anyone else I know. Zoe still can be extremely entertaining and talented at distracting me while I have seizures, but she also has an unusual amount of empathy for people who are in pain and suffering. That's the world she grew up in, and has found joy in it that she spreads to everyone around her. Anna Kathryn's nurturing side has only grown stronger over the years, as she will drop everything to help if any of us possibly need it, while still having a calming presence. As I write this, she is expecting her first child and will be an amazing mother. I would not trade the relationships I have with my siblings now for anything.

Chapter 6

Chemo

There's something very vulnerable about being in chemo. I felt completely dependent on God and my family, too weak to do anything for myself. Though it was me who was in chemo, we all experienced chemo, and everyone experienced it differently.

———•○•———

Little Maggie: My mommy took me to chemo and would stay by me all day at the chemo clinic. I liked it when she held my hand and touched me. It made me feel a little better. My daddy worked late hours because he watched my brother and sisters while I was in chemo.

Kathi: At this point, the adrenaline is gone, I've cried to where I can't cry anymore, different people are watching my other three 3 kids daily, and Rob is working till 2:00 in the morning not able to keep up with work. I'm spending 3 – 4 days a week at the chemo clinic, and when we are home, Maggie is throwing up or having seizures most of the time. I'm cleaning her up, injecting medicine in her port, doing laundry from all the throw-up during the night. When Rob and I would go to bed at night, we would just lie there – with absolutely nothing to say because we both knew where each other's hearts were. We just needed to be.

Rob: Many nights during the week, Kathi and I would just sit in bed and not say a word to each other. She had just spent all day at the chemo clinic for the third day in a row – emotionally and physically drained. I had stayed up until 2:00 in the morning catching up with work. We didn't need to talk or say anything. We were in battle and just needed to be next to each other to gather strength for the next day.

As the oldest child, Dax stepped up and helped often anyways, but especially when I was sick. He took on roles that no 9-year-old child should ever have to. At one point in chemo I was sent home with bags of fluid so that I could stay out of the hospital and get treated at home. My mom taught Dax how to flush my port so that he could help in whatever way he was able to. There was something comforting about having my big brother flush my port instead of nurses in the hospital. Though he was 9, I never questioned his capability.

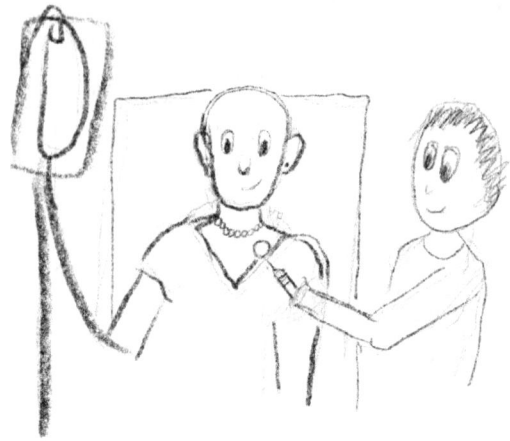

Little Maggie: Dax is my brother and he used to help my mommy by giving me medicine through my port. It made me feel happy because I knew he wanted to help me feel better.

August 16, 2004
   FROM: LaBelle (Grandmother)
   TO: Rob
Subject: Update on Weekend

Did you guys have a good weekend? Was Maggie feeling better? Let me know how you are. I love and think of you all so often.

FROM: Rob
   TO: LaBelle
Dax and I had a good time. Maggie was hooked up to fluids and anti-nausea (via a pump) all weekend. She was pretty much sick all weekend. By 4:00 p.m. on Sunday she was feeling much better. She will have two regular days before it all starts again on Wednesday. They think that it might be like this for the rest of the year.

FROM: LaBelle
   TO: Rob
What is the reason it is making her so sick all the time? Is it an increase in the chemo or because she is wearing down? What can we do for you? I feel so helpless — I can not imagine how it must be for you and Kathi, as well as the kids knowing they can not make it go away. I am so sorry it hurts you all so bad — and Maggie being the most tender and gentle of you all.

I have no wisdom; I have love and prayers and I dream of being with you again. Please really give Kathi, as well as the kids, a real hug and kiss from me. Of course, I send a special one to you, my dear son. God has given you and

Kathi such a special burden to bring him glory — you give Him glory.

I have a new understanding of "My grace is sufficient." It does not stop the pain, but is so strengthening for each moment that passes. His grace will hold us, sometimes a second at a time.

FROM: Rob
TO: LaBelle

There have been no increases in medicine. They have told us that some kids handle induction much easier and then get hammered during the maintenance phase. It's the way their bodies handle it and their bodies just get very tired of the fight.

———————•○•———————

Zoe: Maggie was in chemo when I was about three and four years old. The hardest part for me was watching how sick she got. The way I processed it as a kid was that chemo side effects meant that Maggie isn't okay and everything is suddenly about to change. My parents would (rightly so) need to rush to Maggie to make sure she was okay or to get her medicine. I would panic a lot in moments like that even if it wasn't an emergency because I didn't want her and my parents to leave and go to the hospital again. I was too little to tell the difference between an emergency and a non-emergency. I would often run to somewhere else in the house until it was over. I distinctly remember running and hiding under a blanket when she started getting sick one time, covering my ears and eyes. I didn't want to see it. I didn't want to hear it. It felt like everything around me was shattering if I stayed in the room, in the chaos.

If I wasn't in the chemo clinic, or up all night vomiting at home, I spent many days getting rehydrated in the hospital. I became very weak and it was very disheartening to us all. Even though the chemo was medicine, I seemed much sicker than I was without it. I developed a deep-seated fear of throwing up because of the cycle created during the six months that I was in chemo. I would have a full day of treatment, and then a really difficult night and next few days, which often put me in the hospital to get fluids. By the time I was on the mend, it was almost time to restart the whole cycle. Even the slightest hint of nausea creates a panic inside me that I'll have to go to the hospital and that life will become chaotic.

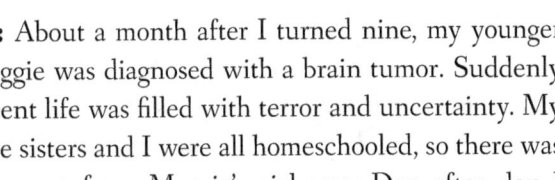

Dax: About a month after I turned nine, my younger sister Maggie was diagnosed with a brain tumor. Suddenly my innocent life was filled with terror and uncertainty. My three little sisters and I were all homeschooled, so there was no real escape from Maggie's sickness. Day after day I watched Maggie vomit from the chemo and my parents weep with sorrow.

Though grieving our old life and worrying about the future, our sense of humor was somehow still intact, if not stronger than ever. At one point, I was given a shirt (which I still own) that says, "hair by chemo, not by choice." It provided a much needed laugh for me, my family, doctors and nurses.

We had a very unique dynamic with Dr. Palmer. He was extremely compassionate but had a dark sense of humor like we did, which really made us bond. We went through a dire period while I was in chemo where we dreaded every appointment with him, as every scan looked worse and worse. At one point we started an ongoing joke that made it a little more bearable. We brought brownies every time as a "bribe" for good news, and told him that if he gave us more bad news we'd spike the brownies with laxatives. Of course we never did, but threatening that made us feel like we had some tiny amount of control in the situation and gave us all a good laugh.

Rob: August 23, 2004

Maggie's oncologist is going to reevaluate her chemo treatment at the six month mark in November. At that MRI scan, they'll be looking for progress on the residual tumor, not just stability. Depending on what occurs, Maggie could be looking at another surgery and other treatment options.

Little Maggie: Dr. Palmer, who gave me my chemo, would give me medicine to help me feel better and would come talk with me in the hospital and in the chemo room. He is really kind and tells really silly jokes. Whenever I would go into his office, he would play tricks on me. I like playing April Fools jokes on him.

Chapter 7

Friends

When your world is unraveling, it's your friends who pick you up and hold you together. This journey would have been impossible in many ways if it hadn't been for the people surrounding us. I was too young to truly understand the extent of the help offered to us by our church, our friends, and even friends of friends. Our family never went without. There were always meals, support, and love.

I also had two very close friends who stuck with me through thick and, well, thick. Ashley, Ariana, and I moved into a newly developed neighborhood at the same time when we were all toddlers, and stayed neighbors for 14 years. Needless to say, I was very close with both of them. When they signed up to be Maggie Bushway's friend at age 3, they did not know they were signing up for visiting me in the hospital on Thanksgiving, or helping me relearn how to walk, or being on the phone with me during a seizure at age 28. I often think of what it must have been like from their perspective, how scared they must have been at times.

———————○———————

Ashley: Maggie and I were inseparable growing up. We were more than just neighbors; we were family. When I found out that Maggie had cancer, we were just 7 years old. This was a lot to take in at such a young age; I was terrified and didn't know how to wrap my head around this horrible news. I would cry in my mom's lap worrying about what was going to happen, I was so afraid of losing my best friend. I knew no matter what, I was going to be by her side through it all. I was at anything and everything I could go to when it came to Maggie; doctor appointments, surgeries, even her Make-a-Wish trip. It was heartbreaking to see my best friend, so young, going through this tragedy, I felt so helpless. Maggie and I would lie together in her hospital bed; talking, laughing, and reading books, everything felt like this would finally come to an end but then she would have another seizure or have to stay in the hospital longer. I prayed God would just take this all away from her. I was so happy when she would feel up to playing outside, seeing her being a kid and having fun meant the world to me.

———————○———————

Both Ariana and Ashley had to face a fear that most don't face until they're much older: that their close friend wouldn't get better or wouldn't come home from the hospital. They both played crucial roles in emotionally supporting me through this difficult time. Ashley went with me to doctor appointments and surgery pre-ops, and Ariana would cheer me up and distract me from those gut-wrenching appointments, and remind me that I was still a child. I will be forever grateful for these two loyal friends who never left my side no matter how hard it got.

Ariana: Growing up with a best friend with cancer was a lot like growing up around someone from a totally different culture than your own. The Bushways' schedule was always packed tight with doctors appointments and errands, and I, of course, just wanted to see my best friend with little to no consideration of how I fit into their plans. I'm sure any family under the circumstances would just want some time to themselves, and yet they always, always had room for one more at the dinner table.

Dear Maggie,

I hope you are glad to be home. I was very happy when Dax told me that the surgery went well. Me and two friends from school prayed for you. I've really missed you. Dax also told me that you were in bed. I hope you like the picture will make you happy. Just remember that we love you, A.K, Zoe, Dax, your mom and dad, and all of my family loves you. Have a great Thanksgiving! - Ariana

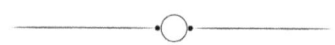

I will always have a special place in my heart for my fellow cancer friends. Only they truly knew what I was going through. I made some friends on the younger children's side of the chemo clinic, but I really bonded with several kids on the teenage side of the clinic too. Out of the fellow cancer patients that I was really close with, I attended 3 funerals. Around the time that I was diagnosed, so was an older man at our church, Mr. George.

———————○———————

Rob: In a room at the back of our church, sat two people about to begin a journey together. Maggie, our then seven-year-old daughter, sat next to George, a grandfather of 5. The elders of our church began to pray that God would protect and heal them as they began their chemo treatments the following week. Over the next two years, God would use that newly formed friendship to build strength and encouragement during some of the most painful times in their lives.

———————○———————

Little Maggie: Before I had chemo, I met Mr. George. We had our ports put in on the same day and we have chemo at the same place.

Losing hair as a little girl was both terrifying and embarrassing. I was warned it would happen, but I still wasn't quite prepared. Once it started falling out, the nurses at the chemo clinic told us it was possible that I could sit up in bed one morning with my hair still on my pillow. The idea of this was really scary to me.

———○———

Rob: Within a couple of weeks of starting chemo, George lost his hair and proudly showed off his bald head to Maggie at church. Tired of pulling clumps of hair out of her own head, Maggie decided that she wanted to shave hers off and be like George. She wanted a little bit of control over what was happening to her.

———○———

If Mr. George could do it, so could I. We went to a family friend's house who was a barber. She was both physically and emotionally gentle about it. By this time I had a big scar on the right side of my head that was still healing. My dad took some pictures during the process, and there's one that will always haunt me. It's a close-up of my face that happened to be taken at the exact moment that it really hit me that I was about to be bald. The tears welled up in my eyes as the scissors snipped off the first strands of a full head of hair and the camera snapped a portrait of that moment.

Before now, just by looking at me, one wouldn't think I had cancer. But in just a few short minutes people would be able to glance at me and identify me as a cancer patient immediately. It was a huge first step on a long path that lay ahead of me.

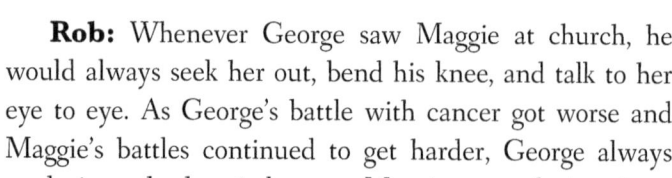

Rob: Whenever George saw Maggie at church, he would always seek her out, bend his knee, and talk to her eye to eye. As George's battle with cancer got worse and Maggie's battles continued to get harder, George always made it to the hospital to see Maggie, even during times when he could hardly drive.

The Lord brought two folks together who couldn't be any more opposite, to be each other's strength and encouragement: a 58 year-old man with grandkids and an 8-year-old little girl. Both aligned with Christ's suffering and walking the blurry line between heaven and earth.

Mr. George grew sicker, and his suffering more noticeable. At one point it occurred to me that he was having more hospital stays than I was, a big feat. Two days before Easter, Mr. George and I parted ways on the blurry line. His suffering was finally relieved and I knew he was where he always longed to be. There was something so beautiful about that Easter Sunday, seeing his wife worshiping at church with the biggest smile on her face. She always exuded joy, but especially on this day. We talked to her afterwards and she said that she was picturing the Easter celebration in Heaven that her husband was a part of and that as much as she was grieving for herself, she was so happy for him.

Little Maggie: Mr. George is in Heaven now. When I see him in Heaven, I'm going to give him a big hug.

Chapter 8

Faith Like a Child

W hen I originally started writing this book at age 8, it was titled *God and Maggie*. Right before my diagnosis, I had just become a Christian. Before really building a solid sinner/savior relationship with God, I had to quickly learn to cling to Him for my life, to daily beg for healing, and to trust that He loved me despite what my life looked like.

———————◦○•———————

Little Maggie: I never knew I needed God before I had Cancer.

I often said that phrase throughout my childhood. I think what I meant by that was that I knew that my soul needed God, but it baffled me how much I was dependent on him for my every earthly and physical need. I prayed for his help during every seizure and scary test or surgery. I didn't realize before this journey how weak and helpless we all were and how we had to 100% lean on God every step of the way. We didn't really have a choice.

Rob: I was taking Maggie to a chemo treatment 2 -3 weeks ago. I was asking her about what God might be teaching her through everything that she has been going through and what she has been learning.

She thought for a minute and then replied, "I think God has been teaching me that all things work out for good for those that love God. He's also been teaching me to pray to Him for very basic things."

At one point in homeschooling, before my diagnosis, our focus with my schooling shifted. I was struggling to keep up and it was clear that I was not able to continue with the same curriculum. Instead of doing the same work that I was having trouble with, we decided to do some memorization. My mom chose Psalm 121 because we both needed this reminder. I don't remember much other school during this time, but I remember working on memorizing this passage frequently with my mom.

. . .

"I lift up my eyes to the hills.
    From where does my help come?
My help comes from the Lord,
    who made heaven and earth.
He will not let your foot be moved;
    he who keeps you will not slumber.
Behold, he who keeps Israel
    will neither slumber nor sleep.
The Lord is your keeper;
    the Lord is your shade on your right hand.
The sun shall not strike you by day,
    nor the moon by night.
The Lord will keep you from all evil;
    he will keep your life.
The Lord will keep
    your going out and your coming in
    from this time forth and forevermore."

I don't know what I would've clung to during chemo, radiation, and long hospital stays if we did not have this time of memorization. During what seemed like endless nights of seizures, I reminded myself that the Lord neither slumbers nor sleeps, and was with me during my sleepless nights. When I was afraid for my life I was reminded that the Lord will keep my life. When I had unrelenting panic due to the location of the tumor, I thought about how the Lord will keep me from all evil.

Little Maggie: I don't remember a time that I was angry at God, the doctors, or everything going on. I was really sad that I had to go to the hospital a lot and that I couldn't see Anna Kathryn, Zoe, or Dax. I was also sad that I couldn't jump or run because everyone else in my neighborhood was running and jumping. But I don't remember being angry.

This is really a testament to how my parents handled everything. They could have easily instilled doubt and anger within me towards God because he allowed this to happen or didn't seem to intervene. Instead they taught me that God intervenes in ways that aren't as obvious. I became thankful for my chemo treatments because my parents told me God provided the medicine and doctors and surgeries that were saving my life. I didn't see the absence of God in my storm, I saw Him as the One handing me an umbrella.

Little Maggie: God really cares and He helps me most of the time when I don't feel good. He made the people who make medicine, and he really does care.

Rob: Seeing Maggie courageously go forward with surgeries, tests, chemo; watching Dax struggle with issues that are extremely difficult, even for adults; observing the effects that this cancer has had on our family; seeing my in-laws and my parents grapple with all of this. God, through all of this, has pricked my heart. I'm beginning to see things through a lens of pain and hurt that I'd never thought possible before and he's using Maggie's circumstances to do it. It's true, you find yourself crying more often, moving slower, and thinking more.

God's people do suffer. But, it is through that path of suffering that He begins to show Himself in ways that many people will never experience. It's a blessing that He is choosing to show Himself in this way and it's grace that He loves us so much to do so.

Chapter 9

Brave

Ironically, as I went through treatments and surgeries over the next few years, all of the adults in my life told me that I was so brave and so compliant. I never understood what they meant because I was terrified the whole time. And I was compliant because I didn't really have a choice. I was too young to make the scary decisions myself, or even be in the know about them. I felt like a fraud when adults would tell me I was brave, because on the inside I was paralyzed with fear, but I was losing the ability to express that fear to others.

My seizures are often triggered by anxiety, and often cause anxiety at the same time. So if I am worried or afraid of something, it will likely cause a seizure. But sometimes one will start out of the blue and make me irrationally afraid over nothing. It could manifest with other symptoms, but also by itself at times. Early on, I came up with a system for dealing with it: I hid in my parents' closet with the lights off and listened to hymns until it passed. Even before we knew specific information about my seizures and their symptoms, I had an idea of what made it better and worse. Sensory

59

stimulation made it worse, so isolating myself in the dark closet helped in that way. Emotionally, giving my mind something else to focus on, like hymns, helped distract me from the anxiety, which in turn, helped break the cycle. I still use this method sometimes. Not in my parents' closet anymore, but I choose a song that I know every word to, (right now it's "Abide in Me"), and will repeat it in my head as I am seizing. It works with other songs, too, but especially when it's a comforting hymn.

One song that was so special to me was "Brave" by Nichole Nordeman. The chorus goes: "Cause it's been fear that ties me down to everything. But it's been love, your love that cuts the strings. So long, status quo, I think I just let go, you make me want to be brave." I would listen to it while seizing and pray that God would make me brave.

———————•○•———————

September 29, 2005

Rob: Maggie had one of the worst nights with seizures that I can remember. The ramifications of cancer are far-reaching. After her seizures passed last night, Maggie and I sang hymns together until she finally dropped off to sleep at 11:30 p.m. Her favorites: "Amazing Grace," "It is Well With My Soul," "This is My Father's World," and "A Mighty Fortress is Our God." Maggie has a lot of the words memorized from choir camp last year, and it is indeed such sweet music to listen to her sing.

———————•○•———————

As a child, you don't understand all of the things that could go wrong. You don't get how high the stakes are, how dangerous every single decision can be. There's a reason Jesus tells us to have child-like faith. I was afraid all the time, but I wasn't afraid of the diagnosis, I was afraid of this thing that I didn't understand but that was rocking my world. Now, I understand everything there is to fear. I've lived it. If I were diagnosed with brain cancer today, I would like to say I'd be as brave. I'd like to say I'd trust God to handle everything. But I know deep down that I'd not be as brave as Little Maggie. I don't think that I'd be as compliant, especially knowing now how terrible chemo was, and how difficult relearning things after every surgery was.

Another special song to our whole family, also by Nichole Nordeman, was called "Gratitude." The song is a prayer asking that God would provide rain (protection, peace, necessities). It ends with: "Or maybe not, not today. Peace might be another world away, and if that's the case, we give thanks to you with gratitude. For lessons learned in how to trust in you, that we are blessed beyond what we could ever dream in abundance or in need, and if you never grant us peace. But Jesus, would you please?" It wasn't that we liked this song because it reflected our headspace. It was that if God didn't answer our prayers the way that we wanted, this is the attitude we wanted to have. We were terrified that God wouldn't "come through" for us and wouldn't cure me. He didn't answer our prayers exactly how we asked, but looking back, we see how we are blessed beyond what we could ever dream, even if He didn't grant us peace.

Pearls

Dear Little Maggie,
I know that you're scared, but you're doing
    great.
You don't think so now, but just you wait.
You'll look back and envy for your faith like
    a child,
And how in your darkest times you still
    smiled.
Stayed strong wave after wave,
Dear Little Maggie, you make me want to be
    brave.
-Big Maggie

Chapter 10

Radiation

Well into a very intense chemo journey, my new neurosurgeon and oncologist met and decided to stop my chemotherapy treatments. My tumor was actually growing instead of shrinking. The months of sickness and misery from chemo were for nothing.

Another surgery was not an option, as the location of my tumor made it too risky. They decided to try a brand new treatment called Gamma-Knife Radiation. It's a laser-radiation procedure and is non-invasive. The neurosurgeon who was an expert at this had never done it on a pediatric patient, making it an unprecedented treatment, but it was my last shot at surviving this battle. The surgeon was in Pittsburgh, so we'd have to travel for it. Thankfully, this wasn't going to be a series of radiation treatments, it would be a one-time-event.

October 12, 2004

Rob: We will be leaving for Pittsburgh on Tuesday, October 26, out of Colorado Springs. Maggie will have pre-op workups on Wednesday, October 27. She will then have surgery at 6:00 a.m. on Thursday, October 28. We will be returning home from Pittsburgh on Friday, October 29.

Kathi and I are more hopeful than we have ever been since this journey began last year. At the same time, we are more gun-shy and weary than ever before. I hope you can understand the dichotomy of those two statements.

Maggie's seizures are back to where they were pre-surgery last year. This is a nasty little tumor. We may not know for several months how effective the surgery was in dealing with Maggie's seizures. It's possible that the tumor may have done permanent damage to the temporal lobe area. If that is the case, we will have some very serious options to pray about. The oncologist is withholding judgment on resuming chemo until after the surgery.

———————◯———————

October 17, 2004

Hi everyone, this is Maggie.

I've been reading my emails from this year and last year. And I've been looking through my things people gave me last year. One of the emails was about people getting up early and coming to the hospital to see me. They are reminding me about everything that happened last year. Thank you for caring about me.

I'm scared about the Gamma Knife and when I'm asleep what they will do. I looked on the computer and watched a little video about the gamma knife happening to somebody. I'm scared that when I'm in the hospital I will have a seizure.

I've never been to Pennsylvania before and I only get to stay there 3 days and I will be in the hospital 2 days. I'll probably be let out of the hospital on the 2nd day and only have 1 day to look around. I'm really hoping that I'll feel better after I wake up and that I won't feel bad in the hospital. Thank you for loving me and sending me cards, bringing groceries to us, and buying our plane tickets.

From,

Maggie

Radiation was a scary thing for us to wrap our minds around. If they succeed, it may save my life. If the numbers were off at all, it would have probably killed me.

Dax was able to go with us, which really put me at ease. It helped the procedure feel more like it was back in Colorado, where my siblings were free to visit me.

My surgeon warned us beforehand, "I have no doubt that I can cure her seizures, I just don't know if I can get the whole tumor." It was my last option, but we really only expected it to improve my quality of life.

October 28, 2004

Rob: Maggie is out of surgery and in recovery. The Gamma Knife surgery went very well. The MRI actually picked up a little more tumor region than the other MRI machines we have used, so the surgeon was able to include that in the radiation kill zone. We were reassured time and again, from everyone that we ran into, that Maggie was being treated by the best in this field. She was pretty nervous, but ready to feel better.

I can't thank you enough for praying for Maggie and this trip, for helping with Zoe and Anna Kathryn while we are away, and for the tremendous outpouring of financial support.

———————————•◯•———————————

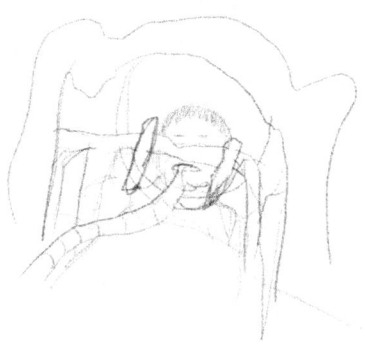

Little Maggie: One day we found out that the chemotherapy wasn't working, so I went to Pittsburgh and had Gamma Knife radiation. I am feeling better but it's hard to not have seizures.

———————————○•———————————

I don't remember much about this trip, besides one vivid memory. In hospitals, especially pediatric units, therapy animals roam the halls. I'd seen dozens of dogs, and some cats, who would come and sit on my lap to cheer me up. But in Pittsburgh, I had a miniature pony pay me a visit. For a long time afterwards, I figured it must have been a hallucination from the meds I was on.

It would take several months of waiting to see if the surgery worked, and in the meantime we hoped and prayed that it was slowly disintegrating the tumor like it should. It was discouraging that my seizures didn't get any better. In fact, they got worse. This didn't help with the anxiety of if it would shrink the tumor, since the surgeon was so sure it would cure my seizures.

Chapter 11

Stages

At first I didn't understand the severity of what was growing inside my 8-year-old brain, but I remember the moment it clicked with me that I could die. Though weak and exhausted, I still was unable to sleep. Staring at the ceiling, well after my family had gone to bed, I started thinking about my chemo clinic friend, Kyrstin, who had recently died. I'd seen her just weeks before, and it seemed so weird to me that she was gone. It also made me grasp the reality of cancer more. I thought about my recent scans showing that the chemo wasn't working and that my tumor was continuing to grow. We were so weary of getting these results time after time. I prayed that God would heal me and make my tumor go away. I added that if He didn't, I knew I would be in heaven with Him and my friends.

It's not that I stopped fighting, but from then on, I wasn't as scared about my situation because I realized that the worst thing that could happen was that I died. And if I did, I'd be with God in glory. Looking back, I didn't realize how much we all thought I was going to die. At my chemo clinic, I picked up on the fact that there were three "opportunities" for kids with cancer that hinted at how bad your condition was.

Those of us who were well enough were invited to a ski trip in Aspen, Colorado, for a week. It happened to fall on my birthday, and I was able to go! It was unlike anything I'd ever done before. All of us kids who usually only saw each other in the clinic while receiving treatments and staring death in the face had the opportunity to play together and actually be children again for a week.

———————○———————

Little Maggie: Miss Jean, my nurse from my chemo clinic, took me and some other kids from my chemo clinic to Aspen for a week and I learned how to ski. It was my first time being away from Mommy and Daddy. I was there for my birthday. I had a lot of fun. I really like skiing because I like to go fast on the big hills and I like turning.

Pearls

When your prognosis is considered critical, you qualify for a wish to be granted by a foundation called Make-A-Wish. After learning that the long months of chemo didn't work and after trying a new type of radiation, anxiously waiting on results, we didn't want to qualify for a wish. But it was an opportunity to do something fun as a family outside of our current situation.

I decided that I wanted to visit the American Girl Store in Chicago. They didn't just send us there, they sent us on a shopping spree. Unlimited dolls and doll clothes and doll furniture. Dax didn't have quite as much fun as me and my sisters, but we made sure to visit some science museums to include him in the fun.

———————•○•———————

Little Maggie: Ashley went with me on my Make-A-Wish trip to the American Girl Store in Chicago. I was not sure if I was going to get to go on my trip because I had been so sick.

Finally, some of us were assigned a photographer who would follow us around in our daily life, in hospitals, and while we're getting treatments. I was assigned Miss Peggy, who was very fun and bubbly. She did photo shoots with my family and made sure we had an abundance of pictures together. The realization of why we had this photographer hit me one day. They want to make sure that the family of the patient has pictures of and with their child if the child dies. I still have all of these bittersweet pictures to this day.

———————•○•———————

Rob: Driving around town, I would plan out Maggie's funeral in my head, practice my speech, and wonder what songs we would sing. I would do that often. In my head and heart, she was always just a day away from death.

Chapter 12

Remission

For a whole year and a half we lived in a cycle of desperation, finding a new treatment, and getting our hopes up, only for the scans to show it didn't work. This Gamma Knife Radiation was brand new technology, and it was my only hope for killing a tumor embedded so deep in my brain. Still, we went into it trying to not get our hopes up.

Three months after treatment, I had an MRI to check on the tumor's size and status. We weren't expecting any big changes to show up since it hadn't been that long yet. We weren't used to receiving good news. In fact, I don't think we'd heard good news since this all started in 2003.

———————————•○•———————————

January 20, 2005
Rob: There has been a 50% reduction in the size of Maggie's tumor. Her oncologist was shocked. He didn't expect to see this kind of reduction so early. This is such

wonderful news, to finally see something positive happening. We have hope again. If you could see my face as I'm typing this...

My nasty tumor that didn't respond to anything miraculously continued to shrink over the months. I don't remember that time period at all; my brain was very busy and my little body was weary from fighting.

Rob: While meeting with Maggie's oncologist on Wednesday, I suddenly began feeling very tired, my eyes felt like closing. I had to struggle to keep them open. This was not the time nor the place to go to sleep!

It occurred to me on the way home that I finally felt like my body and mind could rest knowing that Maggie was going to be OK. Kathi said she felt very similarly while in the doctor's office.

Little Maggie: I remember it was a cold day when I found out I did not have cancer anymore. I was outside playing with my friends and I had had an MRI the day before. I was really nervous about what it might be. My daddy ran outside and told me I was well. I was so happy. No tumor!

I still remember that day, but looking back, it didn't feel real to me. I thought about when we were told that I didn't have a tumor after all, just migraines. It felt like that kind of relief, and I didn't trust it. For a while we had an eerie calm where my seizures let up some, and my body was starting to heal.

Rob: Although we have doubted, been angry, and struggled with emotions that are so difficult to describe, God has and always will be good.

Part Two

Convalescence

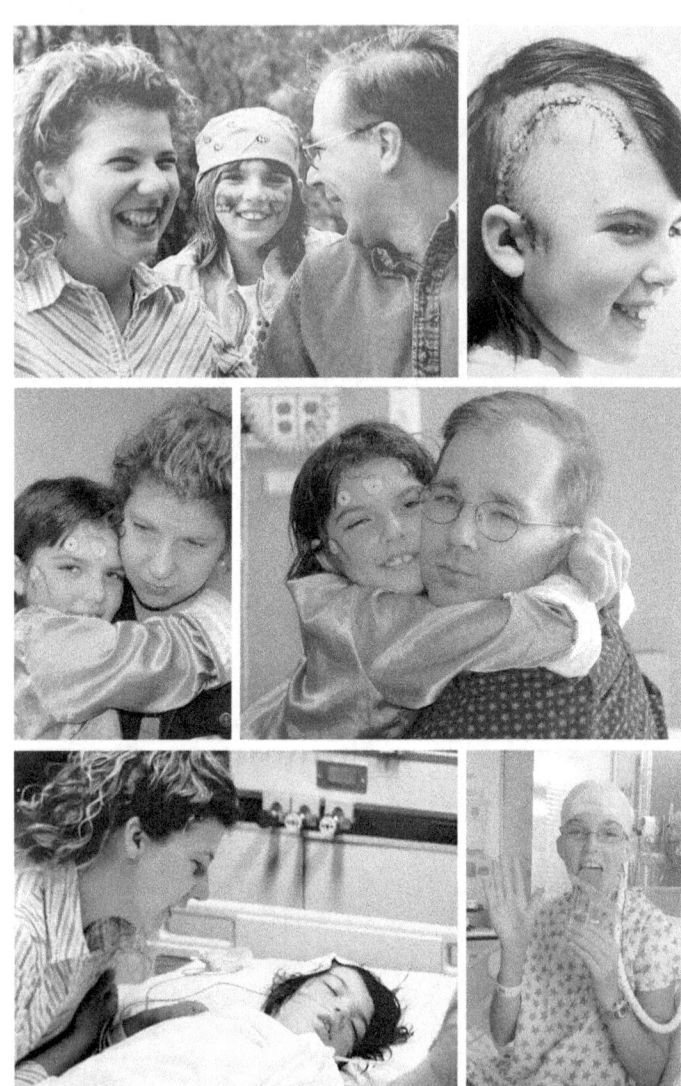

Chapter 13

The Calm Before the Storm

Remission is a strange concept. On one hand, it means you are cancer-free and is such a freeing feeling. However, it doesn't mean you're completely in the clear. There's still a chance that it could come back. You live in an in-between world.

In many ways, cancer is war. I was a prisoner of war, and didn't think I'd ever get out. Then one day I was set free. I ran for my life, knowing that I was being chased. No matter how fast and far I run, I'm still in the mindset of being chased, constantly looking over my shoulder to see if I'm safe.

———————○———————

Rob: This past year has been quite the challenge for me and Kathi. For the first time in several years, there has been no crisis, no emergency trips out of state, no long-term hospital stays, no near-death experiences. It has been really calm and peaceful. Most people would think that it would be pure heaven. However, for us, it's been like crawling around on our hands and knees in the thick smoke that envelops a field after a long fought battle. The heavy gun fire has subsided, and we are thankful to be alive. But as we've surveyed the battlefield, the casualties amongst the platoon are immense; and as we examine our own bodies, we find wounds that run quite deep. We are tired and wounded, but the battle is over.

The casualties stayed with us in the calm. One big casualty was our sense of normalcy. What did normal life look like, again? We had no idea. Another casualty was peace. Our platoon remained on high alert, and honestly it still does.

Zoe: I think everyone in my family suffers from some form or another of trauma from the years of repeated crises. Once things began to settle down and normalize, I had a difficult time adjusting to this "calm," particularly in my teenage years. Learning to live in a more peaceful environment was almost uncomfortable and unfamiliar. It felt eerie. I was always on edge trying to predict when the other shoe was going to drop.

Little Maggie: Sometimes I get a little scared because if I've been having seizures I think the tumor has come back. I have to wait two or three days after an MRI to find out if the tumor has come back again.

I've been in remission for 19 years and sometimes I still get a little scared because if I've been having extra seizures I think the tumor has come back. I have to wait two or three days after an MRI to find out if the tumor has come back again. We've gotten very used to receiving good news, but still wonder if there's some kind of change every time.

We went into radiation with every expectation that it would improve my quality of life, but may not save my life. The benefit to Gamma Knife Radiation was my life, which far outweighs any of the consequences. I do still have a bit of tumor in my brain but it has been dead for 19 years at the time that I'm writing this, thanks to that surgery.

Rob: My daughter has laid in bed praying that she won't have another seizure as she goes to sleep. She's cried herself to sleep countless nights, wishing that her hair would grow back and that people wouldn't call her a boy. It has been a long haul for her and it's not over yet, even with finally being declared cancer free.

After a brief period of calm, we kept waiting for my seizures to be cured too, and after a while they began to get worse instead. I was free of the tumor symptoms, but I had seizures so often, I don't remember most of that year in my life.

———•○•———

Little Maggie: Because I went to Pittsburgh and had surgery, I have to learn new things like how to catch up with people and hot to not be afraid all the time. Dr. Wang put me on some seizure medicine because I have been having a lot of seizures, and I am feeling better.

———•○•———

Chapter 14

The Storm

June 21, 2005

Rob: It's been a while since I've sent an update out on Maggie. She's been responding very well to physical and speech therapy. She's been on new medications the past couple of months and has responded very well to them. She is still on high doses of anti-seizure medicine. She continues to remain cancer-free.

———○———

As my seizures continued to get worse, my doctors wanted to pinpoint exactly where they were originating and where they spread. They set up an extended EEG at the hospital for a week. The hope was that: (1) they were coming from only one side of the brain, and (2) that they were only in the right temporal lobe. That would mean that they could remove it and cure my seizures.

Rob: There is a very high success rate for people who have seizures and who have had this type of surgery, especially when they have maxed out and gone through as many medications as Maggie has. The good news is that a preliminary EEG was done last week and it showed that Maggie's seizures do appear focused around the tumor bed. It is thought that the seizures have been brought on by the tumor being there in the first place and ongoing damage done by the tumor. There is an extensive team that will be involved in reading and studying her tests, so it could be a week or so before we get any of the results.

Maggie will be unmedicated for the next three days, so it will be a rough time for her.

The seizure testing that was necessary for the surgery was pretty traumatic. The medications I was on were holding back a big, scary monster, and my doctors wanted to unleash it. I didn't understand we needed to make it worse in order to make it better. The tests included trying to trigger seizures so that they could capture them on the EEG and give the doctors more information. But to me it was torture, as I had continual seizures the entire time. It didn't make sense to me that they would let me suffer when they had the emergency medicine at their disposal.

June 24, 2005

Rob: They monitored her seizures through a 48-hour EEG and then injected some radioactive isotope at the beginning of one of her seizures. The EEG showed significant slowing around the tumor bed/temporal lobe region, but not enough to definitively say, "she is having temporal lobe seizures." The radioactive isotope, however, showed her right temporal lobe region with a definite red hotspot, compared to her left temporal lobe region, which was a cool blue. Finally, definite proof that she is indeed suffering from temporal lobe seizures — something the doctors have been treating her for but without definitive proof. The tumor caused the seizures and peripheral damage, but removing it didn't cure her seizures.

The next steps were to get a PET scan, and then my doctors would review all of my test results and come up with a plan. But it was more likely than not that I'd have my right temporal lobe removed, which was a foreign concept to us,

Hospitals are a scary place for everyone, but especially for children. For a sterile and safe environment, it sure does feel like you're surrounded by sickness and danger. The "highlight" of hospital stays was always the nurses. We became very well known at our hospital, and were always so relieved to see that I'd be taken care of by people who by this point knew and loved me.

Rob: Maggie's primary nighttime nurse also suffers from temporal lobe seizures and was able to minister to Maggie in some unbelievable ways. Does that confirm to you that God used your prayers to comfort Maggie with a nurse who could understand completely how Maggie was feeling and how she was suffering, and then cater her care accordingly? Our God has always been and will always be a good, all-knowing, providing God.

There are so many people in the world who are going through pain and suffering, but most of the time you only see your individual case. My case was very specific and unusual. Though I was surrounded by family and friends, I still sometimes felt alone because I couldn't relate to anybody. Even my friends at the chemo clinic, or in the hospital weren't fighting these types of seizures. God brought two people together, who share the same kind of pain, so that we both could feel less alone. I thought it was so cool that she had seizures like me and was still a nurse and had a somewhat normal life. It gave me hope.

Healthcare is often about much more than medicine. God provided the team that we needed for my physical, mental, emotional, and spiritual health. Whether it was painting my toenails, providing entertainment, or staying with me so my parents could rest, the nurses and child life specialists went above and beyond what my whole family needed at the time.

Little Maggie: The nurses would come to my room when I was having seizures and rub my legs and play soft music. I really like hymns.

Rob: For the past several years, our family has been on a trek that has been defined by pain, joy, anger, and despair. Watching your daughter suffer through four brain surgeries, six months of chemo, radiation, various therapies, and hope only being answered by disappointment will shake a parent to the core of their soul.

As I write this, I'm watching Maggie suffer through the after-effects of another seizure. They wipe her out. Within the next two -three weeks, she'll be scheduled for a highly advanced MRI that should isolate the hotspot of her seizures. Having that information will likely lead to the removal of the right temporal lobe of her brain.

Chapter 15

Temporal Lobectomy

July 21, 2005

    Rob: We met with Maggie's brain surgeon this week regarding all of Maggie's latest test results. We heard back from him today with the next steps.

After reviewing all of her tests and clinical history, and also consulting with some of the leading seizure testing facilities in the country, he has decided that he needs to remove the right temporal lobe of Maggie's brain. Based on everything that has been reviewed, everyone is certain that Maggie's seizures are coming from that area. By removing that section of her brain, they are hoping for an instant cure. They are viewing the remaining scar tissue as a non-issue and will not be dealing with it at all — unless they find later that they need to.

———————— ·○· ————————

Taking out a lobe of the brain is a serious thing. The temporal lobe primarily deals with memory, though it also processes auditory information, emotions, language, and visual perception. This was incredibly difficult to wrap my 10-year-old mind around. It had never occurred to any of us that you could live without having your entire brain. But we didn't have to completely understand it to trust that this was the next step.

———————○·———————

Rob: The obvious question is: what will Maggie be like after surgery, especially since they are removing such a large portion of the brain. Maggie's side effects will be very minimal. She'll likely have to continue speech therapy, probably going backwards about 6 months in progress. Overall, she should be able to function a lot better with the temporal lobe gone than she is right now. Assuming no mishaps during surgery, no one should be able to tell that she no longer has the right temporal lobe of her brain.

———————○·———————

The majority of the damage that would be done with this surgery had already been done. My temporal lobe was non-functional by this point due to seizures, the tumor resection surgery, and radiation. I might have deficits, but it would help more than it'd hurt. By now, we'd learned that we didn't have real choices. Our choices looked more like: will I have this risky surgery or will I die? Easy decision.

———————○·———————

Rob: When all of this is over, we are planning a big party at our house. Everyone is invited.

To us at the time, my seizures had an expiration date, which was quickly approaching. It was scheduled for August 5th, at 7:30 a.m. The surgery couldn't have come fast enough.

July 28, 2005
Rob: The doctor expects a 3-5 day stay in the hospital. She'll have some pre-surgery workups in the middle of next week. We should have a good idea of the success of the surgery within several weeks. The doctors are approaching this with every expectation that this will cure her of the seizures. However, they are leaving open the possibility that some of the seizure activity could be coming from other parts of her brain. We're praying earnestly that this will be the end of it, and bring closure for Maggie.

We all sat down and talked about the surgery, the risks, and the benefits. I was still just 10, but had quite a lot of experience with medical procedures already.

Initially I was really hopeful that I'd have a good outcome. The rest of my family was afraid to be optimistic.

Rob: Dax's reaction has been more like what Kathi and I have been feeling this past week: scared of hoping, hesitant to believe that it will really work. We feel good about the surgery, but we've become weary and tired, and we've come to expect that things just won't work out the way they're supposed to. I hate to approach this negatively, but that's just where we are emotionally. This past week has been difficult emotionally, with the need to cry always on the fringe.

Before every surgery, doctors are required to warn you about everything that can possibly go wrong. This time I was old enough to understand what they were talking about. Usually surgeons are very confident that none of that will happen, they just legally have to say it. This time was different. I picked up on the anxiety on my neurosurgeon's face, and I understood more that this was risky for him, and that he may have been just as anxious as me, but less anxious than my parents.

Little Maggie: I was really scared before one of my brain surgeries, but I told my mommy to tell the surgeon that it was OK if he messed up.

———————•○•———————

Rob: Walking so close to death for three years will wear you down. The stress of four brain surgeries. Hearing Maggie tell the surgeon that if he messes up, not to worry. She knew he had done his best. Something about that just changes how you live.

We seem to always be tired these past couple of weeks. We are anxious and nervous about what things will be like for Maggie after the surgery.

———————$\circ$————————

August 5, 2005
LaBelle (Grandmother): Maggie's brain surgery should be going on now. It should last until 11:30. There is a slight chance if a small vein near the temporal lobe is over-heated she could have a stroke and be paralyzed. For the last month, she has basically been having non-stop seizures (30-50) a day for roughly 2-3 days at a time, and then a rest period for a couple of days, and then they would be back non-stop.

I am asking for your prayers, to be as our children have been praying since they learned she would be definitely having this invasive 3rd brain surgery. It is "for our Lord to heal her and let her begin a new life or take her home to be with Him for eternity and no longer suffer."

We will all be with her and you can meet her if that is Our Sovereign Lord's plan. He is always on time and His plan is always perfect. THAT is what we have to hold onto. I love you all and bless and thank you for your concern and prayers over these last 2 1/2 years.

———————•○•———————

Zoe: I remember feeling her head after one of her surgeries, and being confused at how soft it felt. I'm not sure I am able to recall how much she changed, other than sometimes she seemed very groggy. I remember us needing to be really careful around her whenever she came home, and seeing her with a head wrap on. I also remember her struggling to understand sarcasm and jokes after one of her brain surgeries.

———————•○•———————

August 12, 2005
Rob: God has been good to Maggie this week.

On Tuesday, around 11:00 a.m., Maggie made a breakthrough. She started playing basketball, doing layups, and walking around the block. The WNBA-style basketball activity came to a halt after the surgeon found out.

Maggie met with her speech and physical therapists this week — they were astounded with what they were seeing: no more tremor activity in her muscles, fantastic processing and logic skills, and ability to hold her attention. These are things that they have been working on for months and have never seen in her before.

Her neurologist has found no neurological deficits and is about as happy as we have ever seen him. Giddy would be a good way to describe his behavior.

Kathi and I are getting very excited. Instead of tears of fear, the Lord has given us tears of joy and they are so wonderful to feel on our cheeks. Pray for us as we begin to enjoy what God has given us and enter into the delicate area of trust. Maggie and the rest of us have hope.

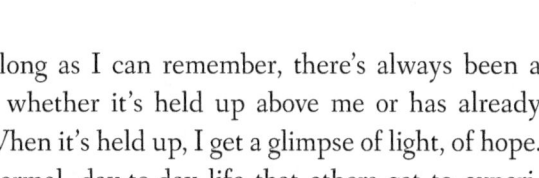

For as long as I can remember, there's always been a giant shoe, whether it's held up above me or has already dropped. When it's held up, I get a glimpse of light, of hope. I see the normal, day-to-day life that others get to experience. I start to get used to it and get hope that this is how the rest of my life will play out. But after a while, it seems like the shoe always drops. My seizures get worse, or I get an extra diagnosis. It's hard to trust the times of peace, health, and hope when it's been a pattern my whole life for the shoe to randomly drop.

After my temporal lobectomy, I initially showed a lot of improvement. We were expecting this to be a cure, so it was very confusing when the other shoe dropped and my seizures came back.

August 29, 2005

Rob: I wanted to thank everyone for your wonderful words of encouragement and support. Most of you have been on this roller coaster ride with us from the very beginning. Thank you.

I also want to let you know that we met with Maggie's brain surgeon today. He thinks that it could be a temporary issue. To be honest, I'm not that confident that it is temporary, but I'm going to pray like a madman that it is. He wants to wait it out for two more weeks and see how she comes along. If she continues to have weeks like she had last week, then he will send her to St. Louis, Missouri, for some invasive brain monitoring.

Chapter 16

Seizures

I didn't have the vocabulary or experience to properly describe my seizures when I was younger. I had them so often that it became normal to me. Over the years, I've gotten better at describing them in imagery and experiences other people can relate to.

I'm going about my day, minding my business, when the feeling hits me out of nowhere. I float in the air with both feet on the ground, an aura of what is about to come. With a sense of dread in my chest, roller coaster sensation in my stomach, and impending electrical storm in my brain, I look for a quiet place to sit and have the seizure. I'm conscious during my seizures, a blessing and a curse.

My hands and feet are the first to show physical signs. My hands tremble, and feet twitch. The right foot twitches side to side, while the left twitches up and down. My limbs join in, too, and, though my limbs are visibly present, shaking faster and faster, I begin to feel my arms and legs in other parts of the room. I can feel my arm, I just somehow feel it on the opposite side of the room.

Sometimes I can make myself stop shaking, but if I do, the floating and separation from my limbs sensation gets much worse. My body also finds another way to continue shaking. If I stand or put weight on my feet, my hands shake faster or my head involuntarily nods aggressively.

By now my heart is racing as if I'm running a marathon. When I track it, I often burn at least 200 calories in the span of the entire seizure. The seizure causes anxiety, and anxiety makes my heart race worse, which causes more anxiety. Distractions, like talking to someone, help, though my end of the conversation may be confusing and slow.

I begin to have false internal sensations that feel so real. Nausea, extreme body temperature, and a very full bladder, are just some of the ways my body tricks me while I'm seizing.

My heart rate usually lets up first, then the others slowly follow. Oftentimes, after 30 minutes, I feel back to normal on the inside, but my hands and feet continue to shake for a while afterwards.

My brain likes a little variety when it comes to seizures. The previous description is my most common one that I've been having for at least 22 years. However, there's another kind that I've only started having in the past few years. Sometimes I hallucinate images that aren't there at all, but most of the hallucinations are distortions of what's already around me. It always starts with what I'm looking at in the moment moving up and down. The paint pattern on the wall will begin looking like it's dripping up the wall. The floor moves like waves in the ocean, making walking around without falling an impossibility. The movements of everything around me get faster and faster, at times eventually to the point where my vision goes black completely. When it gets to this point, I usually fall asleep wherever I am. I've learned to take Ativan as soon as these start, while I can still see my medicine, so that it stops before I get to the blacking out stage.

One of the difficult things about my seizures is that most of the symptoms are internal, not visible to others. So it may look like I'm having a panic attack, or just sitting there during a visual seizure, when I really may need help.

Little Maggie: I have been feeling a lot better and we had a good Christmas. And then the seizures started up. Seizures are when you're shaking and you don't feel good and you just want someone to help you. Usually when I don't feel good, I ask God to help me and he does help, but he also helps with medicine.

Chapter 17

St. Louis

I've had more than enough experience with brain surgeon's for a lifetime. After a while, you begin to see some patterns. Brain surgeons are often egotistical, which can be good sometimes. But a great brain surgeon should also know his limits. The surgeon who performed my temporal lobectomy removed what he felt comfortable with, but left the amygdala and hippocampus because he believed that it was too risky with his skillset and the hospital's lack of equipment needed. However, he had a friend in St. Louis, who he felt could perform the surgery and necessary testing to see how my brain would function if he took out the amygdala and hippocampus.

———•○•———

September 19, 2005

Rob: We received word late this afternoon that Maggie's doctors (her brain surgeon, neurologist, and oncologist) will be sending Maggie to St. Louis for invasive brain monitoring at a seizure testing facility.

Her seizures are not as intense as they were prior to surgery, but they are at least as frequent with much more visible shaking. The doctors feel that the rest of her seizure activity is either coming from the tumor bed/scar tissue or from the little bit of temporal lobe that was not able to be removed.

The testing up until this point had been gluing EEG leads to my scalp and triggering seizures to see in what part of my brain the seizures were located, but they were having trouble picking up activity, as my seizures were coming from deep in my brain.

In order to see exactly where the seizures originate and spread, the doctors decided to implant EEG leads deep in my brain and leave them until they got a good sense of whether or not they could operate.

September 24, 2005

Rob: Maggie can't get to Missouri fast enough.

Maggie has been having heavy non-stop seizures since Thursday night. She spent all day at the clinic on Friday keeping hydrated and medicated, and then heavily medicated with phenol barbiturates since 4:30 yesterday. They have not been able to get the seizures to stop.

Maggie's neurologist has decided to admit her to the

hospital so that they can administer heavier doses of phenobarbital to get the seizures stopped. She will likely be there until late Sunday or Monday.

Meanwhile, the process to get to Missouri is moving along but we do not have a date yet as to when we will leave. The doctor who would be treating Maggie is on vacation next week so nothing will happen until he gets back. I think we will end up driving to Missouri (with the entire family) some time during the week of October 3, and will probably be there for two weeks.

We are rapidly approaching the end of the options available to us to heal Maggie of these seizures. If they find that her seizures are also coming from the other side of her brain as well, there will not be much of anything we can do.

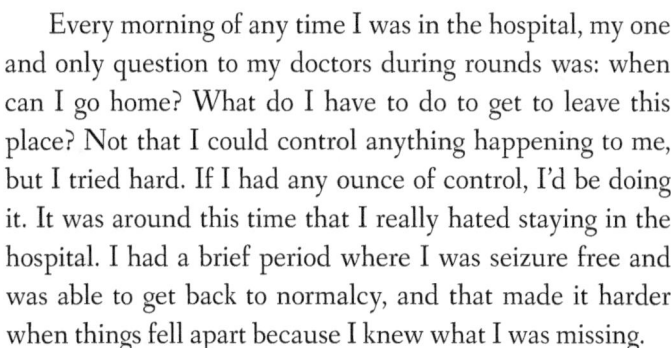

Every morning of any time I was in the hospital, my one and only question to my doctors during rounds was: when can I go home? What do I have to do to get to leave this place? Not that I could control anything happening to me, but I tried hard. If I had any ounce of control, I'd be doing it. It was around this time that I really hated staying in the hospital. I had a brief period where I was seizure free and was able to get back to normalcy, and that made it harder when things fell apart because I knew what I was missing.

September 27, 2005

Rob: Maggie's seizures have not let up much at all since Saturday. She won't be allowed to come home until there are 24 hours of stability. They are looking at giving her high doses of valium or other strong drugs to just get her through to October 10. With these seizures, she can't drink or eat much at all, except during brief spurts.

We found out last night that Maggie's doctors have finally been able to find some documented cases with Maggie's exact problem. There are three adults in California and ten adults in France that had an astrocytoma tumor in the same area of the brain and exhibited her exact peculiar symptoms. Maggie is the only child with a documented case in the world. All of them were eventually cured through multiple surgeries and all of them lived. Everything that has been done up until this point is exactly what needed to be done.

———————————○———————————

Finding this particular blog post was shocking. I know my case is very unique and rare, but I wasn't aware how rare it was. The type and location of my tumor is only found in adults...and in me. My doctors didn't have a case to compare mine with, so they did their best to decide next steps on their own. Finding these cases around the world was a breakthrough and gave us all hope because everyone else was cured after their temporal lobectomies. Even though I wasn't cured after mine, my doctors still hoped that removing my amygdala and hippocampus would do the trick.

September 29, 2005

Rob: They are moving her to Pediatric ICU and will start a Versed drip and treat her with general anesthesia should the Versed drip not work. She is still on a feeding bag, unable to eat much at all. She has several hours of really good moments and then the seizures start back again. At this point, it would not surprise me if Maggie stays in the hospital until we leave for St. Louis on 10/8. If that is the case, Maggie will have spent a solid month in the hospital.

Kathi and I are beyond exhausted. I can't really describe how tired we feel and we have three more weeks to go with two more weeks of a hospital stay. At times it feels like God is giving us more than we can handle, but I know His Word says otherwise and it's that that I need to trust.

God works in mysterious ways. My dad ran a technology blog, and right after I was diagnosed, he began posting updates about me. Sometimes he only wrote about me if we were in a rougher than usual patch. Our family and friends frequently read it to keep tabs on us and to know how to pray. But his readers were primarily tech nerds, which is why what happened next was an absolute miracle.

September 30, 2005

Rob: One of the readers of my blog is at the same neurology conference that Maggie's doctors from St. Louis are at. They got to talking about Maggie and my reader gave them my blog address. The neurologist who will be over Maggie's case started reading the updates on how bad things have been this week and sent me an email late last night. He was very concerned about what he was reading and how things were getting worse. We talked this morning and they arranged for Maggie to be admitted this Monday morning instead of next Monday. We will either be flying out on Saturday or Sunday.

Don't ever doubt the goodness of God, His mercies, and never-ending love for you! He has answered prayers from some of the darkest moments this week and He is providing at the very moment we needed to hear from Him.

———————o○o———————

After flying to St. Louis and getting checked in at the hospital, my new team of doctors came up with a plan. First they'd wean me off all of my medicines so that they could see the full extent of the seizures. This part of EEG Monitoring is always the hardest. Any rare moments of stability I had were only because of my seizure medicines. They were planning on doing neuropsychological testing to see my cognitive functioning level, the EEG, and then an MRI. They also planned on doing an invasive EEG, meaning that they'd implant the leads in my brain and close it up to get a better idea of how deep my seizures were.

October 4, 2005

Rob: They have identified an area in her brain, the hippocampus, that is shrunken and damaged (called hippocampal sclerosis), which they feel is where the rest of Maggie's seizures are coming from. Maggie has not had any really bad seizures since we got here. They are rolling her off the meds pretty quickly, so the really bad seizures that they want to see ought to be coming quickly (tonight or tomorrow).

Wednesday will be decision day. The doctors will be presenting several recommendations and then leaving the ultimate decision on what to do up to us. Regardless, she'll be having surgery on Thursday.

1). Do two surgeries — invasive monitoring surgery, then followed up with a second surgery to core out the tumor bed and remove the hippocampus. There is a lot of risk in this, but it will provide the most data and ensure that they are getting the areas that are responding as a seizure hot zone, as well as address issues involving the tumor bed and hippocampus.

2). Do one surgery — removal of the hippocampus.

3). Do one surgery — removal of the hippocampus and coring out the tumor bed.

Maggie has been in remarkably good spirits today.

The decision was made to do the invasive monitoring

surgery for as much information as possible, and then to remove the tumor bed, amygdala, and hippocampus.

October 6, 2005

Rob: Kathi and I were talking this afternoon about doing something for Maggie when she woke up from her surgery as a way to visibly show how much people love her and are praying for her.

We then began thinking about some of the e-cards that Maggie has been receiving from the hospital this week. The front desk prints them out and delivers them. We then hang them on the wall for her to read and look at in bed. We are also hanging other cards Maggie has received.

So...here is what we are asking.

Please go to this link and fill out the page and submit it. Our goal is to plaster Maggie's four walls with visible signs of people supporting and praying for her. When Maggie returns from ICU to her regular room on Friday, we would love for her to be overwhelmed with all of these e-cards.

In most of the memories I have of hospital stays, I always felt disconnected and separated from my friends and siblings for sometimes weeks at a time. In Colorado, I'd often get visitors and would get to see my siblings here and there, but it was different in St. Louis. My parents were very present and involved, and always tried to make the hard hospital stays easier on me.

I clearly remember parts of this hospital stay because of the overwhelming response to my dad's request. People from all over the world sent e-cards, and the hospital would print them out. My parents read every single one out loud to me. After reading them, my dad would tape the e-card somewhere in my room. The hospital staff began to notice, and it was even on the local news. I made a bet with one of my nurses that if I could completely cover all of my walls and ceiling within two weeks, she'd buy me a new stack of UNO cards from the gift shop. The world took on this challenge too. There were a lot from loved ones, but the majority were from strangers who heard my story and wanted to brighten my day. It made me feel much more connected to the outside world to read these encouraging letters. They were all very heartwarming, and there were also some that brought us comic relief. These are just a tiny fraction of the e-cards I held onto:

———————◦○◦———————

FROM: ZOE BUSHWAY

Hi Maggie, it's snowing we might half to have a hill. I love you and miss you a lot. I'm praying for you.

FROM: RENEE

I know 2 things about you. 1) you have a lot of cool friends, and 2) you have a brain. Good luck with your next procedure!

FROM: JAE (in Korea)

Hello Maggie, I've got news about you. You have a bad disease in your head. So I decided you borrow my power to get rid of your disease. Just give a real strong punch to your disease with my power. After that, please return my power. I know you can win. I'll pray for you!

FROM: WESLEY (Future brother-in-law)

Hey Maggie, how are you doing? I loved playing with you in the Rocky Mountains. Love you, Maggie.

-Weshshshshleayyyyy

FROM: KAREN

G'day Maggie, I just wanted to send you some fairy dust from Australia, so when you're sleeping a big white kangaroo is going to come and jump on your window ledge and deliver it to you so it can make you feel better. You're a brave little girl and a lot of people are praying for you and your family from around the world. Stay strong, princess, and I hope your wall gets covered by Wednesday so the doctor can buy you a surprise.

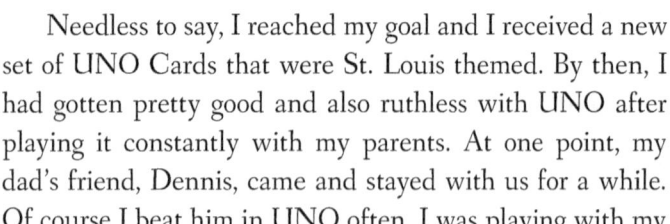

Needless to say, I reached my goal and I received a new set of UNO Cards that were St. Louis themed. By then, I had gotten pretty good and also ruthless with UNO after playing it constantly with my parents. At one point, my dad's friend, Dennis, came and stayed with us for a while. Of course I beat him in UNO often. I was playing with my parents on the side of my bed, but when I played with Dennis, he sat on the end of my bed and we put the table in the middle. What Dennis didn't know was that there was a mirror right behind him, allowing me to see his cards. I found this very funny and even though I was already beating him without this cheat, I didn't tell him until my parents saw in the mirror from my perspective. We all got a good laugh out of it.

Little Maggie: Mr. Dennis came to see me from Georgia and playing Uno and catch with me.

FROM: DENNIS

You hurry up and get better from the surgery, Magonator! I wanna play ball, UNO (if you let me play "Mr. Dennis Wins" again! One day you and I are gonna have to play basketball so I can beat you. PLEASE PLEASE will you let me you??? Love ya, Mag!

The testing to see how well I would function without my amygdala and hippocampus became confusing, strange, and terrifying all at once for us. I distinctly remember a doctor holding a switchboard-looking device. They would flip a switch that "turned off" a certain part of my brain, and ask me to do simple things like reading, identifying my parents, or remembering what state I was in. I happened to have a book set during the Great Depression, so I read an excerpt from that. My doctor interrupted me saying, "why are you reading such a depressing book?" I was growing up in a world where suffering is very normal, so it honestly didn't occur to me until then that it was a depressing book. At least it meant I could still read, though!

Despite having many seizures and a surgery, I entertained myself with poems that I learned before going there. Being homeschooled, we were able to adapt my curriculum to my ability to learn and what I needed to learn at the time. I had recently memorized poems, because memorization was good for repairing some of my brain damage.

Based on the testing, I'd be able to still function normally without my hippocampus and amygdala, so a date was set for the end of the week for the surgery. Dennis was still with us at this point, and he made the day of surgery less scary for me. He wrote "The Magonator" on my door and told everyone, "she will be back." We needed that comic relief because even though the test showed I should still be able to function, it's a very risky surgery and any small mistake could result in more brain damage.

Though I felt very alone during this hospital stay, I was anything but alone. Friends from Colorado rallied around us to support us financially, in prayer, and some even came to visit me. My Sunday School class from church made a giant flower with all of their handprints and notes on it. My dad taped it to the ceiling so that I could look at it while lying in bed.

We also had some not-so-friendly visitors during this hospital stay as well. A hospital chaplain stopped by and at first it seemed normal enough. He told us the story of Jonah, a man who didn't like what God commanded of him, and tried to run away from God. In turn, God sent a large fish to swallow Jonah. After he sat in the belly of the fish for three days repenting, the whale threw him up onto dry land. There are so many possible lessons to get from the story: compassion, second chances, forgiveness, and obedience. What the chaplain told us was that we must have been running from God and this was our fish. We simply had to repent and then all of this would go away. When he left, my parents and I all looked at each other with shock and disbelief. My parents were strong enough in their faith to know that what he said wasn't true, but it still stung. We would've done anything to not be in this situation. Anything.

In the surgery, my doctor was able to remove the amygdala and most of the hippocampus but knew that the rest of it, plus the tumor bed were out of reach without causing major, long-term consequences. My mom recalls falling on the floor screaming, having a sackcloth and ashes reaction to how I woke up from surgery.

———————•○•———————

Kathi: Something happens to the core of your being when you've sent your daughter in for her 5th brain surgery and she wakes up in recovery having seizures. Something has happened when you have finally gotten to the point that you are praying that God will either heal your daughter completely or take her home.

I wasn't aware that this surgery was supposed to cure me of my seizures completely; I thought it was just the next step in continuing to live. My parents, however, went into it with very high expectations and hope, and were just crushed as soon as I started seizing. I, however, was more worried about my face. There was some minor nerve damage to my left eye and left side of my face, making it numb, which felt really strange. In this situation, it was a blessing to not have all of the information that my parents had. Based on the other 13 adults across the world who were like me, I was supposed to be cured. As far as I know, I may still be the only pediatric case, and the only case that wasn't cured by a temporal lobectomy.

Even though my seizures didn't completely stop, there was a big enough improvement after surgery that I was able to go home.

Kathi: As of our last trip to St. Louis Children's Hospital three weeks ago, Maggie remains cancer-free and the doctors are very impressed with Maggie's progress so far. She'll be in various therapies for years to come, but she is the happiest that we have seen in a long time. There is a look in her eyes that has not been there for a long time.

Zoe: Even if we had peace for a little while in the house, I was always waiting for the moment when it would shatter and everything would spin out of control again. I was always trying to predict that moment.

Rob: The bottom fell out this past week, beginning on Sunday night. By Thursday, Maggie's seizures were back with a vengeance. We met with Maggie's neurologist on Friday and will meet with her surgeon early next week to determine what has happened.

This was getting very discouraging and we were all weary of putting all of our hope in a surgery or a treatment, just to be disappointed and have to put our hope in a different treatment. It was such a relief to be back with my siblings, though. Since we were all homeschooled, we were incredibly close and having to be away from them was hard on everyone. It wasn't surprising, but was very difficult when things began to unsettle again.

Rob: Prior to surgery, the surgeon told us that there is a chance that her seizures could also be coming from the scar tissue and this could be a "first effort" at stopping them. He thought that it would be remote, but still a possibility. The last word we received was that removing the scar tissue was not an option due to the risk involved. As has been the case from the beginning, Maggie continues to always be the rare exception.

The disappointment that we all and Maggie have felt this past week cannot be understated. We had no choice but to become vulnerable and believe that this surgery had done its job completely. For Maggie to get a 2-week glimpse at normality and then have it yanked away, just breaks this father's heart.

———————○———————

The upsetting thing about the seizures coming from scar tissue is that all of the things we did to save my life are now causing seizures and are putting my life at risk. Even though it made my seizures worse and more difficult to treat, I have no regrets about having Gamma-Knife Radiation. For a while, the question haunted me: was it really worth it for the quality of life I had? But then I thought about when I was going through chemo. The endless nights I spent throwing up, and days in the hospital getting rehydrated, meant that the chemo was doing its job. I used to thank the oncology nurses for giving me chemo because I understood that this nasty medicine was what I needed. Likewise, the scar tissue represents surgeries that saved my life. Seizures are something that I have to live with long-term, but I wouldn't even be here to have seizures 20 years later, without radiation.

Chapter 18

Foreshocks

Dax: You aren't supposed to have to anxiously wait for the paramedics to come while your little sister convulses uncontrollably, yet such is the reality for lives that cancer touches. It had been seven years of watching convulsions, bloody port lines, and crying because my sister wouldn't wake up. As I stood with my little sisters in the doorway, watching our sister being carried away, I knew that our journey was far from over.

After my last surgery in 2005, I began to have a normal life again. I still had seizures, but they were more under control. I joined a homeschool co-op, allowing me to go to school a few days a week, and I was doing well in it. I especially enjoyed my English class, where I got to write short stories. I wanted nothing more than to be a writer one day, so I took that class very seriously.

One day in March of 2008, I was writing a story for homework, and began to not feel so well. I didn't think it was a big deal. Even after I realized it was a seizure, I tried to just ignore it. Once my hands were shaking so much that I couldn't write anymore, I alerted my mom that I was having a seizure. The next thing I remember is a fire truck and ambulance approaching the house. Believe it or not, we hadn't called 9-1-1 for a seizure until then. Usually we drove to the hospital.

Recently, I asked my sisters what events stand out for them when they think of my cancer/seizure journey. They both said that they remembered the day we called 9-1-1 the clearest.

Zoe: I remember an ambulance and fire truck coming to the house when she couldn't stop seizing one day. That was pretty scary.

Anna Kathryn: I clearly remember this one time specifically, where she was seizing so bad that they had to call an ambulance for her. That was probably the scariest situation that sticks out to me the most. After that time, I think I got more scared each time she had a seizure and thought she would have to go to the hospital every time.

I spent a week in the hospital, and was pretty restless. I knew I was missing school, and genuinely wanted to be there. It took a while to calm my seizures down, but they finally figured out what was making it so much worse. I just started my first cycle the day I had that big seizure. We were so focused on my seizures, we nearly forgot about puberty. My seizures were feeding off of hormones. My care team spent a week trying to get me stabilized and think through all of our options.

When I learned that I'd be in the hospital a little bit longer than Spring Break, it crushed me. I asked for my homework so I could do it in the hospital. School wasn't a burden to me, it was a privilege. I didn't have to do school in the hospital, but when I was able, I got to do at least part of it.

These feelings about school never left. Through middle school, high school, and college, every time I had to miss a class or couldn't do something due to my health, it crushed me in the same way.

———————◯————————

April 7, 2008

Rob: Where to begin...

There are days, and then there are *days*. Today was one of those *days*.

We met with Maggie's neurologist yesterday to go over her most recent MRI, and other tests she's had done. We are still waiting to get results from the MEG test done in St. Louis. Her case is to be presented to the neurology and neurosurgery doctors next week, so we hope to learn some initial results on the MEG then, which we hope will shed some light on the items below.

Here's what Maggie's neurologist has learned so far, based on the MRI, research, talking with doctors in St. Louis, and the tests in which he has performed/ordered.

A volumetrics study was performed on Maggie's brain, and the doctors found that Maggie has about 30% less gray matter in her brain than other children her age. The gray matter includes regions of the brain involved in muscle control, sensory perception, such as seeing and hearing, memory, emotions, and speech, intelligence, and thinking. Maggie's doctor believes that her brain has atrophied across both hemispheres as a result of continual seizures likely caused by the original tumor and scar tissue. We won't know until her next MRI, which will be spread over the next 6 months to a year, if this is getting progressively worse or if it is relatively static.

So Maggie has lost about 30% of the gray matter in her brain, and it is likely being caused by some scar tissue that can't be removed. We won't know for at least 6 months to a year if it is getting progressively worse, and at what rate. Because surgical removal of the scar tissue is an unlikely scenario, Maggie is left with only a couple of options at this point.

1. Continue to experiment with medicines and make adjustments as necessary.

2. Make some drastic changes to Maggie's diet, which has proven to help control seizures, and see what we can do to regulate her hormones.

3. Begin researching Vagal Nerve Stimulators, which present a whole different set of issues. Maggie's doctors have mixed opinions on them.

4. Keep pushing, pushing, pushing

5. Continue praying and seeking God's face, while doing one or more of the above to hold back the atrophy and pray for God to quickly bring about medical advances that can help her.

———————○———————

Part of me wants to know the extent of the atrophy after 15 more years of seizures, but another part of me knows how discouraging the news might be, given that gray matter can't grow back, so I'm at best-case scenario still at 30%, but likely at less now. There are some things that it's best not to find out. I don't know how much more atrophy I have, but I do know that I enjoy working as I'm able, writing, and using my brain for all kinds of creative endeavors. I've found ways to work around memory issues, processing speed, and sensory overload. Knowing an updated percentage would only make me doubt myself and my abilities that I've worked so hard to maintain.

———————○———————

May 10, 2008
Rob: With recommendations from Maggie's local doctors and her doctors in St. Louis, we are proceeding along the following path to bring some level of control to Maggie's seizures: Option 1: Maggie began hormone therapy to limit the interaction between puberty and her seizures. Puberty is definitely causing some bad things with her seizures, which led to the most recent week-long hospital stay. Option 2: Continual adjusting of medicine.

Option 3. Seriously considering a ketogenic diet, which is a modified version of the Atkins diet: no sugar, high fat, extremely low carb. This has huge ramifications for her overall diet, and for our family, but will only last a couple of years. This diet has been known to be very effective in limiting seizures, even after she goes off the diet in two years. Her doctors in St. Louis highly recommended it.

We decided to try the ketogenic diet, as it wouldn't be an extra medication or a surgical option and had many good outcomes from other patients with epilepsy. We found a dietician to help with the process, as it could get complicated. My siblings would eat some of the same things that my parents and I would, but without counting carbs and sugar.

As a 12-year-old, this diet wasn't fun at all. A sausage patty dipped in coconut oil was a regular staple in my day-to-day meals. We'd also have carb-free noodles, carb/sugar free cheesecake, and I'd get frequent spoonfuls of pure coconut oil. Sometimes I'd get a few blueberries for dessert.

My parents said it helped, seizure-wise, but I felt too weak to remember most of it. I lost too much weight that I couldn't afford to lose and was anemic, due to continual hormone issues.

July 15, 2008

Rob: My apologies for not keeping up to date, but things have been quite hairy here the past couple of months.

We began Maggie on the Atkins diet several months ago, and then transitioned her to the full-blown keto diet change last month. We were hoping at this point her energy and affect would be much improved, but other complications are throwing some kinks in it. Hopefully reducing her seizure meds will bring about improvement too.

Maggie has only had one seizure in the past month since being on this new diet, compared to several "noticeable" seizures per week before the diet. When asked about the diet, Maggie said she's able to think better and more clearly.

Benefits from the diet are being blurred, though, by complications with her monthly cycle. She's been on the same cycle for the past month and a half. Her doctors believe there is a direct correlation between her cycle problems, seizures, and her brain issues. She's taking 3 birth control pills per day and iron supplements to help get it under control, and her brain is fighting 100% of the way. Ironically enough, her doctors also believe the diet is helping her cycle not be worse than it already is.

So, with the diet change and her continual monthly cycle, Maggie has had a lot to deal with. She's very tired and has little energy. She seems very dazed and withdrawn. Every so often we'll see a sparkle in her eye, but it has been very rare over the past month and a half.

———————●○———————

Pearls

We tried everything to stop my constant cycle; we even tried to stop puberty from progressing, which didn't work. The rest of the year would prove to be the most challenging time of my life.

Chapter 19

The Earthquake Pt. 1

ugust 7, 2008

Rob: During Tae Kwon Do today, Maggie began having a seizure that needed medical intervention. After treating her with several doses of Ativan, which didn't help at all, we rushed her to Memorial Hospital.

———————○•———————

Tae Kwon Do meant a lot to our family during this time. I was strong enough, and we all just needed to do something normal. Our lives had completely revolved around doctors, hospitals, and separation from each other for so long, so doing something like this together as a family was very exciting.

I'd had seizures here and there during Tae Kwon Do, and had to take it easier than the rest of my family, but this day was different. It got out of control very fast, and despite everyone stopping to help, we had to go to the hospital.

That was the last thing I wanted, especially at Tae Kwon Do. I'd just received my green belt and was strong there; I didn't show my weaknesses there. I could do the splits and defend myself against everyone except my own body.

———•○•———

August 7, 2008

Rob: They have admitted Maggie and will be keeping her until she is stable enough to go home. They will be evaluating her diet, blood work, EEG, and medicines.

Just last night, Maggie took her last dose of Topamax, after going through a three-week weaning period. This is her first "big" seizure since the last time she was in the hospital in March.

It is never a good sign when you begin to know each of the nurses on a first-name basis.

———•○•———

My dad was right, but in another sense it was nice to know my nurses on a first-name basis. I am a complicated case and seem to scare people on their first time taking care of me. These nurses knew exactly what I needed medically and emotionally and also what my family needed. Dax was old enough to know this was bad, worse than other hospital stays. The nurses allowed him to come in and read Psalms to me. I vaguely remember this, but it was such a comfort to me.

August 8, 2008

Rob: Been a rough couple of days.

Maggie had seizures all day yesterday and has had several long ones today. The seizures are now coming every hour and a half. The only thing the doctors can do to get them under control is to give her extremely large doses of phenobarbital.

With all the drugs they are giving Maggie, she's also blown a vein. They are considering implanting another port due to how often she's in the hospital and having to get drugs. She had her previous chemo port removed several years ago.

———○———

After extensive testing, the doctors found that my seizures originate from the tumor bed in the Insular Cortex, but then they travel to the Basal Ganglia. This part of the brain affects movements, causing the type of rhythmic shaking that I have during my seizures.

———○———

August 10, 2008

Rob: I just spoke with Kathi and she told me that Maggie's affect is much better than she has seen in days. We would not be surprised if the doctor lets Maggie go home Monday or Tuesday.

Maggie had such a fun time with her Tae Kwon Do instructor staying the night with her, while Kathi and I got to go home and crash. They watched movies, watched Tae Kwon Do Olympic stuff, and had the closest thing to a slumber party that you can have while in the hospital.

I remember this night distinctly because, although I was in the hospital, it was very special to me to have a sleepover with my Tae Kwon Do instructor, and I know it was good for my parents to get a night at home. I was used to having visitors during the day, but it felt good to have someone who was brave enough to stay with me for a longer period of time and face my night seizures.

August 11. 2008

Rob: Keeping Maggie stable is a challenge. Just spoke with Kathi - Maggie is in the midst of another 3 hour seizure - not as intense as in previous days, but still not a good sign.

Sometimes those types of seizures can be the most exhausting for the person experiencing them. You're aware of everything happening in your body, and because it's not an intense seizure, intervention with Ativan isn't always warranted. It can look like shaking for hours while being alert and talking. At some point you think your muscles are too tired and can't possibly shake anymore, yet they somehow find a way.

--------○--------

August 13, 2008

Rob: Yesterday was Maggie's best day yet, but she still had about three seizures. She had one this morning about four hours long. As soon as they intervene with drugs, it stops. Tomorrow will be one week in the hospital. I'd be surprised if she's home by this coming weekend.

It has been one long week for Maggie. Right now her seizures are as bad or worse than when she was admitted last Wednesday. This morning, the nurses had to give Maggie oxygen to help her breathe in the midst of another 2-hour episode. In the throes of these latest seizures, she is having trouble exhaling and feels like she's choking on something. The oxygen helped her a great deal. It gets more and more complicated as the hours move on.

The doctors are setting up a new test, called a SPECT scan, to give them more information about what is happening during her seizures. This is the same scan that helped the doctors isolate the temporal lobe area several years ago.

Meanwhile, she soldiers on. We are very thankful for our many friends who are helping us during this time with our kids and meals.

--------○--------

We were frequently in the hospital, but I think everyone knew that this hospital stay was different. I typically didn't have trouble breathing during my seizures. Everything was out of control. I don't have many clear memories of it, but I do remember that families from our church who were taking care of my siblings made sure that they got to spend quality time with me. Anna Kathryn and Zoe brought me cards and snuggled with me, and Dax sat by my bedside, held my hand, and wept as he read Psalms to me. I don't think I was responsive at the time, but was aware of my surroundings.

Dax: On a particularly dark day, when it seemed like the seizures would never stop and that my sister would never leave the hospital, her nurse sat with me, wept with me, and prayed with me.

August 16, 2008

Rob: Maggie had a SPECT scan this morning and it showed two to three significant hot spots in her brain, all located around the original tumor bed, which is in the insular region. Two hot spots are right above the insular, another is higher up in the frontal lobe. This is very significant news.

St. Louis Children's Hospital is reviewing the scan right now and will be letting us know if there is anything they can do to help her. We hope to hear later today/early tomorrow.

Surgery in this area is extremely risky, and she would be having surgery in that area twice: once to place testing strips, and another to remove the areas causing her so much trouble. If they decide to move forward, Maggie (along with Kathi and I) will be medevaced out on Sunday or Monday.

Meanwhile, Maggie remains in the ICU while we wait and pray about the next step.

August 17, 2008

Everything is getting set for Maggie to get transferred to St. Louis on Monday morning.

The plan right now, and it could change, is to leave the hospital by ambulance at 9:30 a.m. on Monday. It will take us to the airport, where a medical airplane will be waiting for us. We'll then fly to St. Louis and be transported to the hospital from that airport.

As of five minutes ago, Maggie was not doing well at all. She's been seizing all day, even with a huge amount of Ativan, steroids, Kepra, and other drugs they've been giving her. Her heart rate was getting too high and she was having trouble breathing.

It just makes you want to close your eyes and cry.

August 18, 2008

We arrived in St. Louis about an hour ago. The flight over went really well - surreal, but well. Maggie had two to three seizures while in the air. Maggie is in ICU right now as the doctors make a plan to stabilize her, as well as address the issues causing her seizures.

<u>Caring for someone</u>
-Talk to them even when they can't hear you
-Hold them
-Speak up for them, especially when they can't speak for themselves
-Touch their skin
-Brush their hair
-Clean their glasses
-Cry with them
-Lie down next to them in the bed
-Watch what they want to watch on TV
-Look their nurse in the eye as they speak with you
-Put lotion on their feet
-Leave the room and get some rest
-Bring in their favorite pillow from home
-Read to them
-Find a quiet spot and let the tears flow
-Pray for and with them
-Thank the person who cleans their room and brings them food

August 19, 2008

Maggie wasn't in the ICU for more than an hour when her seizures started kicking in again. The doctors in ICU and Neurology took a very aggressive stance on bringing them under control. 20 milligrams of Ativan in less than 30 minutes - that is a HUGE dose. She has been sleeping ever since.

We met with Maggie's neurologist tonight and he is going to take a very aggressive approach at stopping these seizures, likely putting her in a Versed-induced coma tomorrow. That coma could last several days. They will also begin putting Maggie on a nutrition tube during that time, and watching her respiratory levels closely. Their goal right now is to get Maggie's brain to rest.

August 21, 2008

It took a lot longer and a higher dose of pento-barbital to get Maggie heavily sedated, but she is well on her way. The 4 milligrams of pentobarbital is beginning to do what 17 milligrams of Versed never did. When Kathi and I first saw Maggie after the procedure was done, she was still aware of her surroundings, looking at us, trying to communicate with us, and she knew that a tube was down her throat. It was beyond heartbreaking. However, the sedation finally took effect and they are seeing some good slowing in her brain. They want to see a lot more over tonight and tomorrow. We hope to hear some information on the SPECT scan and MRI mapping tomorrow.

11:45pm:

Well, we met with Maggie's neurologist today to go over their interpretation of the SPECT scan and MRI mapping. First, a quick update on how Maggie is doing.

Maggie is still in her drug-induced coma. She is fighting a high temperature and infection, most likely in her lungs. We'll learn more later tonight/tomorrow on the infection. This is a common problem when people get intubated with a breathing tube. She's sleeping well, though, and her brain is resting. She'll get transitioned out of this coma on Sunday.

Now on to the SPECT/MRI mapping. Maggie's seizures are well focused and not generalized. That means that they are well contained to the right hemisphere in her brain, and are focused on the sensorimotor, frontal, and insular areas on the right side of the brain. The root cause appears to be coming from the insular cortex, near to where the tumor was, but that has to be verified through additional testing.

The doctors don't feel good about their chances of isolating the entire area of her seizures around the insular cortex region. The region is so vast, that they can't safely place a lot of sensors. Assuming Maggie's seizures don't return after she comes out of her coma on Saturday, they want to run an additional test to help make the decision about placing some probes that deep in her brain. That test can only be done when she is not having any seizures. Hopefully a seizure drug, Felbamate, and the drug-induced coma will help her seizures to stop to the point of being able to get that additional test done.

Without being able to place those probes with a high probability of success, surgical resection is out of the question. Assuming that stays out of the question, we move on to options.

The first option is the introduction of a new drug, Felbamate. It's usually a drug of last resort, and Maggie is at that point. She started that drug yesterday and is off all other drugs. It will take some time to get fully ramped up on that new drug.

A next option is a Vagus Nerve Stimulator implanted that sends an electrical impulse to the vagus nerve to help control seizures. It doesn't stop them, but would help control them. That option would be looked at if her new drug proved to be as ineffective as all of her previous drugs.

A third option is a hemispherectomy, where they disconnect the side of the brain causing all of the seizures. Maggie would no longer have use of that side of her brain. Maggie would also lose significant use of her left hand, lose some peripheral vision, and would have to learn to walk again. Disconnecting the right side of her brain would fully stop her seizures, though. We would have to weigh this option in terms of the impact of her seizures on her life and the benefits/losses brought on by the hemispherectomy. This is a most serious option, but it is moving up the list as all of the other options have gotten ticked off.

We will get some second opinions, especially as we get closer to #3. We will doggedly pursue #1 and #2, and other options we may not be aware of right now, before even considering #3.

So, as you can see, the importance of running that additional test next week is critical. It doesn't have to happen next week, but it would be very good to get it done while we are here. The doctors will be very reluctant to resect the area causing all of her problems unless the probability for success was very high. Right now, the probability for success with a resection is looking low.

We serve a sovereign God, who remains in control even when things appear out of control and stacked up against us.

While my parents were experiencing hell, I was somehow experiencing Heaven. I never died during this period, so it was likely a dream. I won't make any claims, all I know is that God comforted my soul as my body was in the fight of its life. My memories of this are hazy but I distinctly remember some parts of it. I was aware that I didn't have my scars anymore and was completely healed. I had been sick my entire childhood, so I didn't know what feeling healthy was like, but I remember feeling it then. I was at complete, seizure/tumor-free peace, walking with Jesus. As my doctors began the process of bringing me out of the coma, I could feel that I was being pulled away from it, and started arguing with God, trying to convince Him to let me stay there. He said that there's things for me to do here on earth. At the moment I didn't care, I just didn't want to go back.

———— •◦• ————

August 24, 2008
9:26am

Rob: So the waiting game begins. The doctors are making their rounds, and then the neurology doctors will come in to give the official OK to bring Maggie out of her coma. Then, we wait and see how Maggie will respond as she comes out.

We got confirmation this morning that Maggie does have pneumonia and a urinary tract infection.

We are very thankful that Mark and Christy Watson, our friends from Tupelo, have driven up to be with us this coming week. As Wednesday approaches, it'll be 3 weeks since Maggie was admitted to the hospital.

9:52pm

Maggie is still asleep, but is showing some good activity in her brain waves. It'll probably be late tonight/tomorrow morning before she starts to wake up.

Waking up from the coma was like sliding down a long black tunnel, slowly going back to awareness of my surroundings. The first thing I was aware of was that I had multiple tubes down my throat and felt like I was suffocating. Once they took the tubes out, I managed to say "I want to go back" over and over again. Nobody knew what I was talking about, and I couldn't explain. I just was very insistent that I was not supposed to be here. I didn't belong in a world where I woke up from perfect peace to me still seizing, my body fighting infections, and still being separated from my siblings. Nothing was okay.

Chapter 20

The Earthquake Pt. 2

August 27, 2008

Rob: Maggie's seizures continue on. However, for today, they appear to be calming down a little. She is very weak and fragile right now. In addition, her entire right peripheral vision is getting impacted when a seizure starts. For the first 20-30 seconds, she is unable to see anything on her right side.

The physical therapists have been by to help Maggie with a lot of muscle tightness. Maggie also got out of bed a few minutes ago, and is getting her hair washed. We'll be taking a short trip to the rooftop garden later today, which will be a huge change of scenery for her.

———————————————•○•———————————————

While I was seizing during the whole hospital stay and don't remember much, there's a night that I'll never forget. The pneumonia resulted in a dangerously high fever. Honestly, I don't remember feeling any sicker than I had been from the seizures alone, but I was very aware that there was something wrong because everyone around me was panicking. The room was filled with nurses and doctors who made an assembly line to get ice water to my room.

I was very confused because I didn't feel hot or like I had a fever at all, so I didn't understand why they were making a big deal out of it, and just felt more cold than anything. But I was scared because everyone else was scared. At one point it dawned on me that everybody thought I was about to die. My life had been on the line for weeks, but it felt very real this particular night. As I was thinking about this, I became aware of someone lying in bed next to me. I looked over and saw nobody, but heard a whisper in my ear, "I will never leave you or forsake you," over and over the entire night. This calmed me and helped me realize no matter what happens, I'm still in the presence and protection of God.

My mom told me later that I was in a vegetative state when this happened, and they weren't sure how aware I was of my surroundings. They'd had so many people ask them how to pray for me, and they said to pray that whether I was aware of them or not, that I'd at least feel God's presence.

———————◯———————

August 28, 2008

Rob: When I left the hospital tonight, Maggie was fighting a 105 degree temperature from an infection. When I called the room later tonight to check in, the doctors had gotten it down to 103. They put Maggie in isolation as they keep the environment as controlled as possible to beat the infection. Maggie is continuing to have a very, very difficult battle.

August 29, 2008

Rob: Things have settled down a little this morning, improving upon the criticality of last night/early morning. Maggie's temp is back down to 100, but she is extremely weak and not very responsive to questions, movement, etc. She is mostly answering questions with her eyes.

The doctors have ordered a slew of tests to get at the root of this infection. Her pneumonia, though, appears to be improving. She's had about four seizures this morning, but the large, jerky movements have gone away.

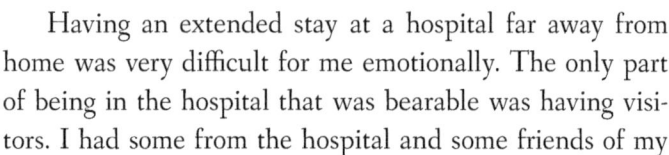

Having an extended stay at a hospital far away from home was very difficult for me emotionally. The only part of being in the hospital that was bearable was having visitors. I had some from the hospital and some friends of my parents visited, but nobody my age.

At the beginning of September, I was staring at the calendar trying to make sense of it. I thought it was still early August. When I realized it was actually September, the first thing I thought of was that I missed my friend Ashley's birthday. Then I thought of everything I must be missing at home. I started panicking and feeling a strong urge to just leave.

September 1, 2008

Rob: Jeffrey from our church took pictures of people holding up signs expressing their love for Maggie — they are so precious. The pictures came in at the perfect time — right when Maggie was breaking down about how much she missed home. She cried nonstop, and these pictures brought true smiles to her face, pointing to people and calling them by name.

———————○·———————

After being in the hospital in this state for so long, we began to lose hope that we'd ever leave. My room was right by the helicopter pad, the very one I landed on when I arrived. As the helicopters would start to take off, my parents would try to get the attention of the pilot by banging on the window saying "take us with you!" Of course they were (mostly) joking, but it comforted me that my parents wanted to leave as much as I did.

At first we would pray that I'd stop seizing, then that we'd be able to go home, but at one point we just started to pray for Jesus to come back. We knew that even if I make it through this, even if we're able to go home, we'd have to face these seizures forever, or until Jesus comes back. I'm sure it seemed very dark to everyone around us to pray for the end of the world, but that's just where we were at mentally.

There was something that brought a smile to our faces in these dark days. One day when we were all exhausted, depressed, and afraid, my dad was on YouTube and came across a video of someone sledding off of their roof. We went down a rabbit hole for hours. It didn't fix anything, but we'd do anything to laugh again.

———————•◯•———————

Rob: We played several of the videos you all have created. They proved to be great medicine. You guys are the best. Thank you for bringing laughter into Maggie's room.

Maggie will definitely have the Ictal SPECT test on Tuesday. Once radiology decides when to bring the tracer up, there will only be a two to three hour window when it will be effective. That means, sometime during the two to three hour period that the tracer is ready to be injected, they don't want Maggie to have any seizure activity. Given her level of seizure activity, that will be very difficult. If it doesn't work out for tomorrow, they will try again on Wednesday. This is a very, very important test.

September 2, 2008
Rob: The scan is done, and now we wait for the results. During the scan, Maggie was the stillest we've seen her in a month. She has not been seizure-free for this amount of time (outside the coma) over the past month, and it began to happen exactly at the point we needed it to - last night through this morning. It is amazing to see, and a real testament to the people praying for her. Thanks be to God.

———————•◯•———————

I was starting to make enough improvement to get out of my four walls, even if it was still in the hospital. They had a rooftop garden that I'd visited last time I was admitted in 2005. Being able to visit it, even just for a few minutes, gave me hope that I'd be able to leave soon and that there was still an outside world.

September 3, 2008

Rob: The second SPECT scan was done today, but it will likely be a day or two before we get the official results. Meanwhile, we are moving forward with the Vagus Nerve Stimulator implant later this week/first of next week. The Vagus Nerve Stimulator is the next step that has to be tried, as well as offering the least risk. We'll learn more about remaining options after we get the SPECT results in the next several days.

<u>Next steps after the hospital:</u>

It should go without saying that the past month has been extremely trying - what I like to call "living in all shades of gray."

The good news is that Maggie is much better than when this all started. She is doing so well that the doctors are considering releasing her on Friday. She'll have the VNS, (Vagus Nerve Stimulator) implanted Tuesday through outpatient surgery.

The Vagus Nerve Stimulator is a chest implant with a wire running up my vagus nerve into the brain. Every few minutes it would send electrical impulses to the brain to prevent seizures.

September 3, 2008

Rob: While we wait to see how effective the VNS and new seizure med will be, the doctors have begun preparing us for the real possibility of a hemispherectomy - disconnecting the right hemisphere of Maggie's brain. We don't know if that will be weeks, months, or years away, but it is becoming more and more clear that this is likely where things will end up, as we have exhausted all other options known to us and Maggie's doctors. Much of this depends on how the new drug works, how helpful the VNS is, if we can keep Maggie out of the hospital, and if they can get more solid info from the interictal SPECT test for a possible resection. The doctors are not hopeful about a possible resection, though. There is a lot more risk of something going wrong during the resection, which would cause much more damage and no benefit, than a hemispherectomy would.

Once we get home and recover from this past month, we'll begin the process of seeking second opinions. We'll also be talking to parents of kids who have had hemispherectomies, praying for Jesus to return quickly, and ensuring that we have not left a single bridge untraveled.

Even though I was scheduled for a VNS surgery in a few days, they discharged me since I was doing well enough. When we left Colorado, our mindset was just on getting me to St. Louis, so we weren't really thinking about packing for what to wear on the way home. I had the outfit I wore there, but no shoes. So first thing that day, we went to the mall to get shoes, then we spent a day at the Botanical Gardens. Besides visiting the rooftop garden, I hadn't been outside since the beginning of August. It felt good, but very strange.

September 9, 2008

Rob: Maggie is now in surgery, and will be finished in about 2 hours.

Update 1: 9:09 They just called from the operating room, and are beginning to close up. Maggie is doing fine.

Update 2: 9:25 The surgeon just came by and told us everything went fine, and that Maggie is in recovery. She probably won't feel the stimulator at the setting it is currently at, but will over the next several weeks as the doctors increase the electrical current. The doctor made two incisions: one is in the neck to wrap the wires around the vagus nerve, and another near her left shoulder to insert the VNS device.

The VNS surgery was minor, and I only had to stay overnight. We were so ready to go home, so we were out of there as fast as possible. There was just one issue. My bladder hadn't quite woken up yet from the surgery. We went to the emergency room, anxious about what this would mean and praying that they wouldn't try to keep us. It wasn't long before my bladder work up and we were on the next flight home.

Chapter 21

Faith Like an Adult

Even while my body was slowly healing after I came home, it took my mind and soul so much longer to heal. After experiencing that state of peace, the immediate and continual suffering in my life after waking up weighed heavy on me in the following weeks. I couldn't understand why God would show me what it could be like and then let me wake up still having non-stop seizures and to be on the brink of death for weeks on end. I felt like He rejected me, and I felt very disconnected from my faith for the first time in years. I felt close to God through this terrifying journey, even in St. Louis, but not during this time. Though I wasn't suicidal, I was constantly thinking about Heaven and comparing it to my present reality. Everything about the earth seemed dead. I hadn't told my parents about my experience in the coma. I thought that it would be too much or that they wouldn't believe me because I didn't die. But I began to worry about my depression and decided they needed to know. They reacted so lovingly and believed me. We talked about how God can comfort you like that when you're very sick, even if you don't die, and that God didn't reject me, it just wasn't my time. Telling them helped, but I still felt spiritually abandoned.

After this conversation, my parents asked an elder from our church to come talk to me and help me work through these feelings. He opened his Bible and read 2 Corinthians 12:7-10. He told me that Paul was sick, too, which he referred to as a "thorn in my flesh," and begged God to take it away, but God didn't. Instead, He told Paul, "My grace is sufficient for you, for my power is made perfect in weakness." The elder told me that even though God hasn't taken away my thorn in the flesh, He will use it to accomplish great things and that His grace is all I need. He actually uses weak people the most, and my weakness makes me strong.

That was the biggest breakthrough in my walk with the Lord to date. I have looked back on this passage numerous times when I'm going through a rough patch with my seizures. The first part is so comforting to me, but I've always prayed that I'd get to a point one day where I can actually boast all the more gladly in my weaknesses.

———————•○•———————

September 25, 2008

Rob: Over the last five years, one of the most frequent questions I get asked is "how do you and Kathi do it?"

It is absolutely nothing but God's grace. I know that sounds all flowery and "Christianese," but it is the truth.

- It is God's grace and favor that He withheld from us and Maggie how difficult a road this would be

- It is God's grace that He is still withholding from us what things will be like six months from now
- It is God's grace that He provides us a little bit of light at a time. It could be nothing but darkness.
- It's God's grace that He brought Maggie to Himself at an early age
- It is God's grace that Maggie is not suffering more than what she is
- It is God's grace that He has provided a people to carry Maggie and our family in prayer, while His plan is flawlessly being played out.
- It is God's grace that He chose Maggie for this.
- It is God's grace that He uses His church body to love and provide for us. He doesn't have to.
- It is God's grace that He is using this to grow Kathi and I closer to each other than further apart. Believe me, this is not the norm.
- It is God's grace that He is being faithful to grow Dax into a man that seeks to walk in holiness rather than bitterness
- It is God's grace that Anna Kathryn and Zoe exude joy and beauty.
- It is God's grace that Maggie has doctors who love her and refuse to give up on her
- It is God's grace that we even have hope
- It is God's grace that Maggie has continued to worship Him in humility, peace, and contentment. The more she suffers, the more she longs for Him. That is nothing but grace.

His grace is sufficient for us.

Chapter 22

Aftershocks

April 27, 2009

Rob: Over the past several weeks, folks have been asking me about Maggie and how things are going. The statement that pretty much summarizes everything is that things remain predictably unpredictable. Maggie has had an awesome week so far, but the last 3 - 6 weeks have been up and down with 2 - 3 seizures a week. The good news is that the combination of the Vagus Nerve Stimulator and an increase in Maggie's seizure medicine is helping lessen the intensity of the seizure and the post-ictal phase of the seizure. That means we are able to keep Maggie out of the hospital and manage it from home. That is a huge win.

We've also started experimenting with returning to Sunday School, followed up by worship service afterward. Late last year, we made the decision to only attend one hour of church due to the problems that a lengthy time at church and overstimulation was causing Maggie. She seems to be handling it well and is even helping in a 9-year-old Sunday School class.

———————•○•———————

I still struggle sometimes with going to church. I feel strongly that I should attend, but my brain makes it very difficult. I have seizures easily when I wake up early anyway, even if it's to do something quiet. Sometimes when I go, I selfishly feel like I'm risking my health going to church, so I should be rewarded by getting to stay. It doesn't work that way.

I never want to be a distraction, so I try to sit near the back so I can leave the sanctuary if need be. Usually, church starts slow and quiet; my speed. But as the service progresses, the music gets more lively, which is where things go south. My heart starts racing, and my left big toe and right hand twitch. Before the hand joins in, I usually think that it'll be a small one and I won't have to leave. Eventually, my arms and legs start shaking, and that's the latest I should get out.

In 2008, churches didn't livestream, but it's a blessing to have that option now. Of course, it's ideal to have a church family be a part of a body of believers who support you. I was part of a church then and am part of a church now that doesn't shame me or pressure me to come when I'm not feeling well, but when I am there, they rejoice.

———————•○•———————

April 28, 2009

Rob: Maggie has had a rough couple of days and the doctors at Denver Children's Hospital want to admit her tomorrow morning for at least a couple of days for stabilization, monitoring, and testing. Maggie is not at a crisis point, and she is doing OK at the moment, but that could change five minutes from now, though. Please pray that the doctors will learn something that will likely help Maggie so that things will not continue to slowly get worse.

This extended EEG hospital stay felt very strange. During my last hospital stay, every day I was fighting for my life. Now, I felt well enough that I didn't think I should really be there.

April 30, 2009
11:24am
Rob: The doctors begin weaning Maggie off of her meds tonight to see if they can get some better information on the EEG...could be a rough couple of days.

8:09pm
Maggie is dealing with the med weaning quite well. In fact, I think she is feeling better. Not exactly what the doctors are looking for, but we'll take what we can get.

May 7, 2009
Rob: We never know what to expect going into a hospital stay and this latest one was no different. They come without any notice and are quite wearing for us all.

We had a really good heart-to-heart/lay it all on the line

conversation with Maggie's main doctor today. A lot was said, but the long and short of it is that barring any medical breakthroughs, surgical intervention, or Jesus coming back to save us from the curse of this world, the long-term reality for Maggie is that this will be a lifetime struggle. This struggle will be a roller coaster ride of wonderful peaks and very painful valleys. There will be many experiments with medications, lots of tests, last-minute and lengthy hospital stays, and lots of various therapies helping Maggie to cope with this life that God has ordained for her.

Though this was extremely difficult to hear, it was a little refreshing to have someone plainly lay it out for us, without giving us any false hope or thinking that they could be the doctor to cure me. And they were right, so far it has been a lifelong roller coaster. But this honest conversation gave us permission to stop trying to constantly find a cure and to redirect to finding the right medicines and VNS settings to manage the seizures. And that's what we've focused on ever since then.

Part Three

Pearl Formation

Chapter 23

Chronic

When I made it to college I felt like I had overcome everything I was told by doctors I would never be able to do. At 17, our family moved from Colorado Springs to Tupelo, Mississippi. Though I loved Colorado and leaving was incredibly difficult, it was also a clean slate. I was starting to feel defined by my medical past and like I would never be able to make a name for myself apart from surviving cancer. In a way, starting over, beginning college, and having my seizures relatively under control felt like a resolution to my story. I saw that part of my life as being over. I thought that if I made it this far, the rest would be easy. But life isn't easy for anyone and certainly wasn't for me.

After feeling a strong calling towards writing my whole life, I began to hone in on my interest in screenwriting and filmmaking. I was able to quickly find a community of independent filmmakers in Mississippi who knew nothing of my past. They mentored me and began to respect me for my merit, not out of pity, which was a fear I always had. Besides the occasional trips to my new specialists, I didn't think about my health much anymore.

I remember the moment I first felt it all slipping away. I was reaching to grab something off of my closet shelf and felt electricity shooting down my arm. It really rattled me but stopped after a while. I felt similar sensations in my hands and feet every once in a while, but it wasn't consistent enough to make a big deal out of.

The following year was a very exciting semester for me. I had completed my first year of college while living at home, which went so well that we decided that I was ready to live on campus. At first, it was a huge success and I was thriving on my own. Little things started happening in the spring semester that didn't seem related to each other at the time. My hands would often tingle and I was feeling more and more zaps. I began experiencing extreme pain in my feet that would literally stop me in my tracks.

One day, I was headed to a class to take a test. Out of nowhere, I could have sworn my feet were on fire. I had to sit down where I was, take my shoes off, and look at my feet to try to convince myself they weren't on fire. It should have been a relief to me that they weren't, but it made me feel like I was insane. Knowing that nothing was outwardly wrong still didn't make the pain go away. I wound up missing that test because how do you simply walk to class when your feet are on fire? You don't; you sit down where you are and cry, praying for the strength to get back up again.

Walking around campus soon became impossible. Sometimes my feet were on fire, but sometimes I was walking on shattered glass. My body would act as if I were actually walking on shards of glass under my feet, constantly adjusting them based on what part of my foot

164

hurt most on the last step. Sometimes they were tingly, and other times it felt like I was getting electrocuted. This, of course, affected all aspects of college, but the area that affected me the most was Film Club. I was Vice President at the time and was always working on short films. For anyone who has been on a film set for even a day, it's obvious that it's physically taxing and you work very long hours. Everyone gets tired and everyone's feet hurt. I really tried to push through it and tell myself that I was in no more pain than anyone else. The best comparison to trying to function and work through this kind of pain is that it's like trying to focus while someone is screaming in your ear. At first, it's just faintly in the distance and you can distract yourself, but the stronger the pain (the louder the scream), the less I'm able to function, let alone think. As the screaming in my head got to an intolerable level, I stepped down from directing a few of the short films, but couldn't bear the thought of stepping back altogether. I never felt more alive than when working on a film, and I wasn't ready to give that up.

Up until this point, I'd only told a few people in Film Club about my pain because I didn't think anyone would believe me. Who would? But after I began having the same painful sensations in my hands, I realized that I was getting very limited in what I was able to do in film. At this point, I couldn't even write on paper without breaking down in tears. The only aspect of filmmaking I don't enjoy is acting. I've never been good at it, and am always too aware of the camera. But I volunteered to play an extra, though only if I'm able to be in a wheelchair. I didn't have a wheelchair, but the school did, and let me borrow it. For this particular film, I was playing the part of a disabled character, but the production ended, and I found that I was able to function on a much higher level that whole week because I used the wheelchair so much. I asked the school if I could start regularly using it to get to classes, and they kindly allowed it.

The way my social circle reacted to me using the wheelchair was eye-opening. I thought that it was glaringly obvious to everyone else how difficult that semester was for me, and how my body quickly became very fragile. But once I was seen using the wheelchair just in my normal classes, some told me I didn't have to stay in character. Others said that I shouldn't be using it because nothing was wrong with me. And I had no clue what was wrong with me, just that something was. But in the back of my head, I was starting to believe that it might just be in my head. It didn't help that I tried to only use the chair about half the time at first, because the times people saw me walking, they either thought I was all better or that they caught me pretending to be disabled. My closest friends knew how much I struggled to sometimes get out of bed, and offered to push me to my classes since my hands were also hurting. My professors were more than accommodating, and helped me figure out the logistics of getting to class, and keeping up with assignments, and also were understanding about days I wasn't there.

Meanwhile, I noticed a concerning progression of the pain: it hurt for anything to touch my skin, (full body), even just the wind or the breeze of someone walking past me. It hurt for my clothes to rub up against me. I had to stop giving people hugs, or really have any form of physical contact with them. I found there is no nice way to set boundaries for this with people. I'd try to say, "Please don't hug me" or "It hurts to touch," but people just didn't understand, and often would get offended or think I was being rude. There was also the frequent situation where someone would hug me before I had the chance to ask them not to. Then they'd feel bad when I would tell them afterward. It was a tough social spot to be in. I was able to finish the semester with a lot of help from friends and professors.

I was seeing an epileptologist in Memphis, and his best guess was that it was a long-lasting side effect of radiation. We decided to get a second opinion from a local neurologist, which was a huge turning point. It's always so hard to find a new doctor, especially a new neurologist. He wholeheartedly believed me when I told him about my weird "skin hallucinations," which I didn't expect at all. He was interested in my case and also in this new mystery. He believed it to be nerve damage, but that there was usually a root cause of the nerve damage that we'd have to discover. I thought surely it had to do with seizures, brain damage, or the cancer treatment. It really didn't occur to me that I could have something else wrong with me. Because God only gives people one disease in a lifetime, right? And I'd already been through mine. The rest of my life was supposed to be a breeze.

But just like that, we were on the diagnosis hunt again. Last time, it was my parents advocating for me, and I'd go along with whatever everyone else thought was best. As a 20-year-old, this time I was much more involved and informed, with my parents' support in whatever I decided to do.

As I was starting a new semester full of academic tests, I also was going through many medical tests, such as blood samples, nerve conduction tests, and a skin punch biopsy. While we were waiting for results, a brand new symptom revealed itself: my bladder abruptly stopped working altogether. There's no pushing through something like this, or simply telling yourself you can empty your bladder if you try hard enough. I saw a urologist and they hooked us up with a catheter supply company and taught me how to catheterize myself. I wasn't a pro at this, and often needed help at first. I decided it was finally time to move back home. This felt like a huge low. I grew up a fighter, and this felt like I was retreating and giving in.

When my tests came back, we found out that I have Peripheral Neuropathy, a type of nerve damage that affects nerves outside of the brain and spinal cord. This can impact sensory, motor, and autonomic nerves, explaining the pain, tingling, and sudden bladder issues.

Getting a new diagnosis is always hard, but it was also validating this time. Neuropathy can cause weird sensations, such as bugs crawling up your legs or your hands being on fire, which can make you feel crazy. Getting a piece of the diagnosis felt good, but I still had a long road ahead of me. Peripheral Neuropathy is usually caused by something else, which we eventually learned was Sjögren's Syndrome.

Sjögren's is a chronic, autoimmune disease that attacks the parts of the body that produce moisture and causes nerve damage. I felt weird about this diagnosis. I was so incredibly relieved that it had nothing to do with my tumor or seizures. It felt like a weight had been lifted off my shoulders. And I was thankful that I finally had answers and would get treatment. But I was weary of hearing that I'll never completely get better. I'd been told that so often growing up, and couldn't believe this would also be a life-long struggle. It didn't seem fair that I should have to deal with a whole other health issue. Thankfully I was able to get on treatment and manage the symptoms better. My pain is always still there on some level, but on the right medicines, the screaming isn't as loud.

After moving to Mississippi and getting a whole new care team, I learned so much more about my Vagus Nerve Stimulator (VNS). My settings were very low because I couldn't tolerate anything higher. It vibrates on the vocal cords and was very uncomfortable. It saved my life and I will be forever grateful for that, but it wasn't doing much for me at this point. My new doctors decided to turn it up to a higher level, which was still uncomfortable, but I wanted to give it a try.

They also decided to increase my seizure meds. My doctors in Denver had one goal: to get me off all of my seizure medications. Of course, it'd be nice to be at a point one day where I could function off of my meds, but it was unrealistic. My new doctors were more direct with me and didn't give me false hope. It was no longer about curing my seizures and getting to a point where I have no health issues and I'm not dependent on meds. Realistically, it's about managing my lifelong seizures with my VNS and meds.

In 2017, a newer and smarter model of the Vagus Nerve Stimulator came out, and I was among the first people to benefit from it. When taking out my old device, the surgeon said it was barely functioning and had been that way for a while. He believed it was also misplaced the first time, which explains why it hurt so much to use the magnet. So getting the new VNS was like getting it for the first time again. This one has two new functions that are game-changers for me. One: it senses when I'm about to have a seizure or am having one, and sends electrical currents to my brain to try to stop it. It doesn't always stop it, but prevents it from being worse or as long as it would be without it. And when I swipe my magnet across my device, it sends a stronger current which usually helps. Two: it tracks how many seizures it stops or prevents, and makes the information accessible for my doctor. For example, I'll go to the doctor and say I'm having a few seizures a week, but he'll scan my device and it will show that it's stopping about 100 a day.

It's great that it stops them, but that's 100 that start or happen in the background of my brain without me knowing it. It explains why all throughout the day I zone out, can't remember what I'm doing, or frequently have interrupted sleep. This doesn't mean I'm having more than I was before I had my VNS upgraded, I am just more aware now that I'm having multiple kinds of seizures and that my VNS often intervenes before it gets out of hand. It will also tell if I'm having more seizures in the morning or at night, so when my doctor is adjusting my medicine, he knows what time of day to increase the dose.

Most of my appointments don't revolve around getting answers anymore. I've accepted that we've gotten all of the answers we can for the location of my tumor and type of seizures. My appointments are all about management and stability. I can't make the seizures completely go away, but my doctors are always adjusting my treatment to reduce them.

In my junior year of college, I was able to transfer to The University of Mississippi, forty-five minutes from home. My grandpa gifted me with a mobility scooter so that I could get around campus. I truly believe if it weren't for my grandpa doing that, I wouldn't have received my degrees. It was the best gift I've ever received. Between seizures and nerve pain, it took much longer than usual to get through my bachelor's degree. I was really hard on myself and constantly had to come to terms with the fact that my life isn't going to look like other people's. It was okay to take my time. It was okay to drop hands-on classes that I couldn't physically do. It was okay that I missed a lot of classes because I could barely get out of bed. But it wasn't okay to me. I function normally enough that I forget sometimes that I'm missing parts of my brain, I'm constantly having some level of seizure activity, and my immune system attacks parts of my body. I can't hold myself to the same standards as others. But I often do.

The college campus lifestyle was ideal for me. I can't drive, so living on campus and in a small town meant that everything was scooter-distance or a handicapped-accessible bus ride away. I learned after graduating that the real world is not as accommodating as college can be, and there were very few jobs that I could physically do. Upon realizing this, I reluctantly applied for disability benefits. I knew it was necessary, but it felt like I was giving up. However, while in this process, a job came my way. It was for The University of Mississippi but required me to be in grad school. Ask anyone in my life, and they will confirm that I swore I'd never go to grad school. It took me so long to finish my bachelor's degree, I just wanted to be done with college and start working. But if it meant I'd get to start a job in media sooner and get more specialized training in documentary filmmaking, I was interested. Since my seizures were manageable enough at the time, it was doable to go back to school. Around this time, my disability application got approved, even with my new job, so everything was falling into place.

2020 wound up being the strangest year to start grad school. Because of the COVID-19 pandemic, my job was remote, and some of my classes were as well. The circumstances were very difficult, but the option to work remotely worked in my favor the first year. Although I am being treated for my nerve pain, it's still a very present part of my life. There are days when being on my feet is truly a victory, and during this time, being on my feet was very difficult. Had I not been remote, I don't think I would have been able to continue in the program. My thesis was a documentary on Long Covid, which I also happened to be going through. Thankfully, I was able to interview people all over the world virtually, which was a huge blessing.

While I was trying to adjust to my neuropathy being worse, it felt like my brain held it together long enough to graduate, and then things went south with my seizures. I started having a new type of seizure right before grad school started, which was more dangerous, but only happened occasionally. After I graduated they became much more frequent. They'd start with a hallucination; usually, things around me looked like they were moving. A common one is that the paint on the wall looks like it is dripping up the wall, defying gravity. Slowly everything becomes more distorted and moves faster and faster until everything goes black. At this point, I'd either fall asleep or try to get to my bed. While living alone, it was not safe to do this, as I'd usually wind up falling. I've learned with these, that if I take Ativan as soon as it starts, I don't black out anymore.

After grad school, I started doing videography and video editing independently, which gave me a lot of flexibility to work when I'm up to it and take breaks as needed. I was still pretty stubborn about living independently, so I'd go back and forth to my parents' house whenever I needed help with seizures but was sure that I'd get back to the point where I could live alone. At one point, I was getting bad infections from my immunosuppressant and they was causing too many significantly dangerous seizures. This made me finally realize that I couldn't completely care for myself, but that it doesn't diminish my worth or make me less of an adult. I don't have to keep trying to prove to myself that I can be just like everyone else. We built a tiny house in my parents' backyard, so I could have my own space and sense of independence, with them close by to help.

I used to think that the seizures and chronic pain were keeping me from fulfilling my purpose in life, but I think they are guiding me to fulfill the plan God - not Maggie - has for my life. I hope that this book is the first step in that direction. I know many of you read this book to learn my success story where I beat the unbeatable, but I hope what you take away from it is that even though I have chronic conditions, my life is still beautiful and that looking back, I can appreciate everything I've been through and see that it's just part of a much larger story.

Chapter 24

Am I Weak Enough Yet?

May 14, 2024

This wasn't supposed to be the ending of *Pearls*. I'm meticulous about planning, and I extensively planned this book, but I didn't plan for this news. Yesterday, I was diagnosed with Myasthenia Gravis, the autoimmune and neuromuscular disease that my mom has, which causes weakness in the skeletal muscles and eyes. My eye doctor first brought up the concern a few months ago, as my vision changed drastically within a six month period and I randomly needed bifocals at age 28. I wasn't convinced, but I soon began to notice patterns similar to what my mom struggles with.

If I exert myself, my whole body shakes (differently than it does with seizures). The past six months have been extremely difficult, energy-wise. At times, I've thought I'm depressed simply because I find myself in bed so often. I've called myself lazy, wondering why I can't just do what others can, and why everything is so exhausting. Nobody else has to lie down after running a quick errand. I have some swallowing issues, sometimes droopy eyes, my feet drag easily, and I struggle to make and keep facial expressions without the muscles in my face twitching.

Still at the beginning of this journey, I fear for how this will affect my career and passions in the future. I already have had no energy to film the stack of short film scripts that I've been saving to make when I feel better. Will I ever be able to even work on film sets again? Never working those thrilling, but long, hard hours on sets for the sake of art sounds terrifying to me, but it doesn't mean that my purpose has been taken away from me. My passion might be filmmaking, but my purpose is to glorify God and enjoy Him forever. I can do that just as well or maybe even better through writing or video editing, which I'm also passionate about.

As I've seen how this disease has impacted my mom's life, I wonder if I will be able to handle it as gracefully as her and if I'll be as brave as Little Maggie was when facing the terrifying unknown. Will we be able to stop it in its tracks before it progresses further, or will it be a long process? I think back to Paul's thorn in the flesh and how God says His power is made perfect in weakness. But only a day after this diagnosis, my raw and confused prayer is this:

"Am I weak enough yet? Aren't brain cancer, seizures, Sjogren's Syndrome, and nerve pain enough? I understand that suffering is part of my story, but haven't I gone through enough already? I'm sure You could fulfill Your purpose for my suffering with the amount of weakness I already have. But You allowed me to have a lifelong weakness disease on top of everything else. How weak do I need to be?"

———————————— ◯ ————————————

Rob: Just as a pearl takes years to develop, the beauty of pain and suffering may not be realized for years to come. To fix the irritation or wish it away, will rob you of the joy of seeing the pearl of God's priceless purpose in it all.

I think about how I began on this journey 21 years ago, getting a scary diagnosis and just taking it one step at a time. So much has happened in those years, and now, after every daunting test and every painful treatment, I'm able to look back and see the pearls. My prayer is that when I'm 49 and looking back on the 21 years that passed, I can see a whole string of pearls; my suffering made beautiful through Christ who guides me through it.

Afterword

Rob: When my mom died in 2014, it was the first time I had ever felt untethered; the way a little child might feel when they've lost the secure grip of their mom or dad in a crowded mall. Or like how a boat that has lost its anchor just drifts wherever the wind or storm takes it. Or like how a string of pearls that has been cut loses its sense of belonging and suddenly becomes lost. Alone. Purposeless. Vulnerable.

It was some time after the funeral that my sisters and I began the hard process of packing away some of my mom's things. Seeing her clothes, jewelry, handwritten notes, Wedgwood china, and smelling her unique scent all through the house stirred up so many emotions, like the way hearing that old Def Leppard song immediately takes you back to the sights and sounds of your junior high school hallways and cafeteria.

I was in the living room sorting through some of her knickknacks when I spotted her old-English rolltop desk. It was one of my favorite pieces of furniture growing up. There were plenty of drawers, mail slots, and cubbyholes to stash away all kinds of stuff that one wasn't quite ready to get rid of yet; and holding onto stuff was something my mom was very, very good at. In the bottom drawer of this old desk, my mom had tucked away something I had no clue she had, nor would I know how much I would come to need it. It was an anchor back to my mom and an anchor back to a very painful past I had emotionally walled off. It was an anchor back to a story that Maggie would need to read and then write for herself 21 years later.

As I pulled open the bottom drawer, I noticed a Walmart grocery bag jam-packed with printed emails and blog posts all chronicling my family's journey through Maggie's battle with cancer and seizures. What I had come to find out later was that my mom would go to the library every day to check her email and visit my website to read and print the latest update I had posted about Maggie, what our family was going through, and how God was showing Himself to be Sovereignly good, merciful, but not safe.

I still have some of the articles and emails I wrote, but the majority of what Maggie included in her book is the result of my mom's steadfast love for me, my wife, and her grandkids. They are a physical reminder to the legacy and imprint my mom left on those she loved, pursued, prayed for, cried over, witnessed to, and hugged.

That rolltop desk now sits in my office. I inherited my mom's wonderful gift of holding on to little treasures. In those cubbyholes and drawers, I've tucked away notes that my kids have written me, my dad's Vietnam Veteran's hat, Legos that my kids and I built together, and a framed, dried flower that lay on top of my mom's casket.

Acknowledgments

First and foremost, I'd like to thank my parents, Rob and Kathi Bushway, and my siblings: Dax Bushway, Anna Kathryn Watson, and Zoe Marchant for both living this with me and reliving it with me. Thank you for your beautiful contributions to this book. Zoe, your illustrations brought Little Maggie to life, and I'm so thankful for your work.

Thank you to my grandmother, LaBelle Copeland, for printing off and saving all of my dad's detailed blog posts, which made this memoir possible. Thank you to my grandfather, Gerry Copeland for holding onto those after her passing. And thank you to my aunt, Rachel Knight, for your editing skills and encouragement.

I could not begin to make a list of the friends who supported me and my family during our most difficult times. Thank you to all of those who prayed with and for us, brought us meals, and frequently helped take care of my siblings.

I want to thank Ariana Johnston for contributing your perspective on our childhood and for continuing to walk with me in the ups and downs of life. And thank you to Ashley Hosey for your companionship during difficult times, and for your contribution to the book.

Thank you Ginny Robinson for your encouragement, advice, and emotional support as we both explored the process of book writing.

Finally, I am indebted to Barbra Gemar, who first taught me how to write, and helped me start this book in 2004. Thank you for giving me the confidence to write a book as a child, and for giving me confidence to finish it 21 years later.

About the Author

Maggie Bushway is an author, filmmaker, and journalist who resides in North Mississippi. After surviving childhood brain cancer and still living with seizures and autoimmune diseases, she uses her pain to tell stories that give hope to other people in pain. Whether through short films, documentaries, writing, or content creating, pain and hope weave in and out of her storytelling.

For updates about *Pearls: A Memoir on Childhood Brain Cancer and Hope*, go to authormaggiebushway.com.